KING SOLOMON SPIRITUAL LIBRARY
THE GOD ENCYCLOPAEDIA WORD OF INFINITY

BY
THE HOLY SPIRIT OF THE FATHER GOD
THROUGH HIS SERVANT
HRM KING SOLOMON DAVID JESSE ETE
(King Solomon Spiritual Library)
Eteroyal Universal Family -BCS

*All rights reserved
Copyright © Solomon ETE, 2008
Solomon ETE is hereby identified as author
of this work in accordance with Section 77
of the Copyright,
Designs and Patents Act 1988*

*The book cover picture is copyright
to Solomon ETE*

*This book is published by
King Solomon Spiritual Library
P O BOX 27394
London E12 6WW UK
www.kingsolomonspirituallibrary.com*

*This book is sold subject to the conditions
that it shall not, by way of trade or
otherwise, be lent, resold, hired out or
otherwise circulated without the author's or
publisher's prior consent in any form of
binding or cover other than that in which it
is published and without a similar condition
including this condition being imposed on
the subsequent purchaser.*

*A CIP record for this book is available from
the British Library*
ISBN 978-0-9559801-2-1

Content

Chapter One   7-68

THE POWER MIGHTY

A: Introduction   9-35

B: What You Don't Understand Is What I Will Reveal Today
35-43

C: Many People Are Afraid Of Satan   43-50

D: Every Power Come From The Father God   50-55

E: Elementary Gods   56-57

F: God Out Of Good Self Of The Father Almighty   58-59

G: I Am The Power Of All
Powers   59-62

Conclusion A: All The Powers In Heaven And On Earth Are With The Christ Of The Father God Almighty   62-64

Conclusion B: The Supreme Word Is Everything   64-65

Conclusion *C:* The Power Mighty In The Blood Of The Supreme Word Of The Universe (Christ)   65-68

Chapter Two   ***69-176***

THE SUPREME ALTAR

Introduction: 71-73

A: What Is The Meaning Of Altar   73-83

B: Who Altar Who 83-101

C: The Supreme Holy Spirit Needs You As A Home
 101-111

D: What Happened To Adam And Eve   111-126

E: Your Positive And Negative Self Is Inside Or Outside Of You
 126-138

F: Your Position Of Life And Dead Soul Reveal   138-154

G: The Cause Of Your Positive And Negative Instincts, Emotional Actions And Sensations
 154-160

Conclusion A: The Door To Your Soul   160-163

Conclusion B: Negative In And Out – The Fornication Act Of Sexuality   164-170

Conclusion C: Positive In And Out Is The Word   170-176

Chapter three   *177-196*

With Love   177-184

Read Seven Lectures   185-188

List of the Father's Talk   **189**-196

Chapter One

THE
POWER MIGHTY

FATHER'S TALK
(GOD PRESENT)

Christ Our Lord, Eight Judas Iscariot, FATHER Two Thousand and Eight (OH.OC.OH) (Saturday, Eight March, Year Two Thousand and Eight (08.03.2008))

In the Name of Our Lord Jesus Christ, In the Blood of Our Lord Jesus Christ,

Now and forever more

THE POWER MIGHTY IN THE BLOOD OF OUR LORD JESUS CHRIST

Today, it pleases **ME, THE FATHER GOD THE CREATOR OF THE UNIVERSE** to give this wonderful lecture for today. The title is – **THE POWER MIGHTY IN THE BLOOD. THE POWER MIGHTY IN THE BLOOD OF THE SUPREME WORD OF THE UNIVERSE:** *DESCOR CONCIUM RASTY FIAS-OUT* – **THE DIVINE INVOCATION.**

A: INTRODUCTION

THE BLOOD OF THE SUPREME WORD – THE POWER MIGHTY IN THE BLOOD OF OUR LORD JESUS CHRIST

I know that a lot of human beings are doing all sorts of things connected to **BLOOD**. Today **I** want to reveal **THE POWER THAT IS IN THE BLOOD OF THE SUPREME WORD PERSONIFIED OF OUR**

FATHER ADAM WHO CAME INTO THE WORLD AS OUR LORD JESUS CHRIST THE KING OF KINGS AND THE LORD OF LORDS, and also why Satan uses blood to confuse many people.

People drink blood of animals and another human being and they think that is accepted by **THE FATHER GOD THE CREATOR OF THE UNIVERSE.** Every human nature is aware that **THE SUPREME WORD** is everything created and that is **LIFE**. Now we are talking about the **BLOOD** which is also **LIFE.**

There are three things that make life exist physically. Life is managed well physically when these three things are in one and are with one voice and in corporation. The three things are the **Spirit**, the **Blood** and the **Water.**

The power, the energy radiates in the blood. The blood is the middle. In the body the **WORD**, which is the SPIRIT is there, the water is there and the blood is there but the blood maintains the two of them to be alive. Without the blood, life itself will have problems. The water has problems because the water is negative. The water wants to consume the whole body and cause problem in human system, but the blood is very powerful and fights against that. The blood maintains the body for the SPIRIT to live in the body. Then when the SPIRIT has access to live in the body, the SPIRIT now takes care of both the blood and the water in the body.

The blood is one of the greatest phenomena in the system of life.

Therefore, the worst thing you can do is to commit murder. The worst thing you can do to yourself soul is to have anything to do with blood. Shedding blood categorizes you as the worst enemy and that is what **I THE FATHER GOD** hates the most. What **I** cannot forgive you is taking life, because when you shed blood, you are in trouble with **ME** and your soul, no matter how much **I** love you.

Do people know that going to war and killing people for whatever reasons puts you in trouble with **ME, THE FATHER GOD THE CREATOR OF THE UNIVERSE?**

Are you in enmity with **GOD**? You are enemy of life when you kill. When you plan to be wicked to someone whether in dream or in the physical for any reason, you are enemy of life,

You are enemy of **FATHER GOD**.
You fight directly with **FATHER GOD ALMIGHTY**.
You are against the **SUPREME WORD**.

Life is a product of the **SUPREME WORD** because the **WORD** is life. Don't you know that you are fighting **ME, the WORD,** when you tamper with life? You are challenging **ME, the WORD** if you plan evil against any living soul, no matter the reason? That is what **I AM** revealing today. Woe to any murderer and anybody that has anything to do with blood of another innocent human being, because there is **POWER MIGHTY IN THE BLOOD** that is organized by **THE SUPREME WORD.** Not the blood of animal though. As a matter of fact, eating

animals and the slaughter of animals is a sort of punishment to animals, because animals shed blood too much. When you read the lecture – **_THE SUPREME FUTURE_** – and also **_THE BUDGET OF THE FATHER GOD_** – you will see the instructions given therein.
Every human being must be a vegetarian.
All animals must be vegetarian. Every living soul and every living creature must be vegetarian.
You cannot be alive and eat life. You can only consume living organisms such as plants. They are for supporting life. They are the body of the life. You can only consume things that life produces which have body but no soul. Therefore, as human beings the food you should consume are fruits, herbs, leaves and

vegetables. Do not consume lives that have soul.

When you consume lives that have soul you are in enmity with **GOD, THE SUPREME WORD, THE MAKER OF LIFE AND SOUL,** I will set and seek every blood that you have a hand in to your soul. Satan knows this and capitalizes on it. So, the first thing Satan wants every human being to do is to commit the offence of the blood that is, to kill. That is the reason the first negative man on earth was vampire, because he was negative. He was the first man that killed the first man that died. They were Cain and Abel respectively. That is, Cain killed Abel.

Cain was the first wicked human being, while Abel was the first peaceful righteous human being that Cain killed.

The first evil spirit soul was Cain. When Cain eventually died he became the first evil spirit which inspired all wicked and negative human beings on earth. This spirit of Cain, which is evil spirit also known as demon is the first witchcraft spirit, which Satan uses to parade everywhere and do wickedness to people.

The first Holy Ghost that **I** use to inspire and to identify good spirits soul and good things in people is Abel – Abel's spirit. So, there are these two ghosts – the Holy Ghost and the evil ghost called demon or witchcraft.

All evil practices including the secret societies practices, and evil invocations, pass through witchcraft, which is the spirit of Cain, before they can do anything evil. Do not allow anybody to fool you that the secret society they belonged to does not kill anybody. They are lying. People kill for you in that society to survive. And when people sacrifice on your behalf, you get the same punishment, because that is your agent. That is what **I** reveal today.

The entire secrets are in the Records. **I** know everything about what people do in this world. Seven people sit down and plan evil in different countries. They are called Decision Makers in their spiritual nature. People do all sorts of evil things thinking that **I AM THE FATHER GOD** does not see them, but unfortunates to them **I AM THE SUPREME WORD** who created them and live in them.

The secrets of the world are in **MY** hand in the spirit. It is not physical. **MY SPIRIT** possesses someone and that person knows everything about what you sit down anywhere to do. It is just a matter of opening the script and the person sees you. Have you not seen that everything is naked in the eyes of a mad person and so reacts when he or she sees someone with high spirit? Nobody can hide in this world! It is the **SPIRIT WORD** that manipulates everything.

Therefore, **I AM** now revealing that those who have something to do with blood, directly or indirectly, you are in trouble with **ME** your **CREATOR** whether you believe it or not. You are a wanted soul. Forgiveness does not extend up to there. You killed and so you shall be killed. **I** will seek for the blood of Abel in the hand of this generation for eternity. Do not therefore make a second mistake. If you kill, you shall be killed. If you plan wickedness on anyone, wickedness shall follow you. That is the reason **I** brought this Revelation, this Lecture.

I, THE SUPREME WORD OF THE UNIVERSE became flesh and had blood and water. I used **MY** Blood and Water as the final-final sacrifice. **I, THE FATHER GOD** never looked for sacrifice and **I** have never looked for blood, ever.

When you hear that people offered sacrifices to God, it is not for THE FATHER GOD, but for angels. Angels are like small, small energy of GOD. It's like having a motorbike or motorcycle that would not convey a lot people at once compared to say a vehicle that could carry a lot more people and would travel at much higher speed. Angels can also be compared to small engine that can only generate power equivalent to small batteries or a generator that produces small current just to carry may be ten watts of energy to shed a little light. Or the energy could be like that of small flashlights to just about see with. None is like the bright day electricity of God - the super bright day light of God.

What energy, what type of sacrifice – what type of energy can you produce for **ME** to be able to burn one day's sun and to give everything life. Is it not stupidity for any angel or any spirit even human to tell you that **I, THE SUPREME WORD OF THE UNIVERSE, THE FATHER GOD, AND THE CREATOR OF THE UNIVERSE** need sacrifice or that God needs your blood? Which God? Tell **ME!**

Electricians and those dealing with electronics know the meaning of watts and current. They know such things as, when you increase the volume of a radio, the battery dies quickly. Those who use energy to produce light know that the more light you use, the more energy you consume. So, what blood, and what energy can you human with your sinful nature produce for **ME** to use for a day's light? When the sun itself is the visible energy of **MY** generating power, the fuel that the sun uses for one day to light the whole universe is immeasurable. How much energy of blood can you give **ME** to use for that? That means even if you have to kill everybody on earth, still the energy will not even come close to one minute of the sunshine **I** give for mankind.

That shows that every human being is ignorant and elementary. Mankind is stupid and elementary thing that has no understanding, unless of course you learn from **ME, YOUR CREATOR** today.

I brought out this SUPER teaching - this Revelation - this Lecture for mankind to correct their steps. Do not say it is too late and ask – why now and in this generation? Those who came before **ME** are thieves and robbers. Do you think you have any previous knowledge? **I** always allow man to reach their wits end before **I** bring out **MY** wisdom.

Blessed are those who accept this truth. **I** do not need blood. **I** do not need any energy from anybody. **I AM** the energy **MYSELF.** Super sun – the fuel of the super sun for one second that maintain one day's light in the whole world, you cannot produce. **I** produce **MY** fuel for twelve hours and **I** use it for twelve hours. The day **MY** fuel is not enough, the weather that day becomes muddy. You would then see rain and everything else but the sun.

I produce **MY** energy for some area and **I** burn the day out for some people at some other area. **I** had a Lecture on that.

Therefore, no human being should allow Satan to say to you to offer sacrifice. This can only be if you are not positive. All those who support the spirit of Lucifer – the spirit of Cain, they have no access to **MY** Supreme energy of **LIFE**, *LOVE* **AND** *PEACE*. So they are looking for small- small things to do and called sacrifice. Those are demons and you will perish with them.

I know that mankind needed salvation and Satan wanted everyone to perish once and for all. So, because of the sin, which is the virus that Satan put in Adam and Eve **I, THE SUPREME WORD** decided to use the house of Adam to come back. I called **MYSELF** our Lord Jesus Christ, the **WORD**, and Emmanuel.
I was the person that came to die, so that the **WORD** became flesh. So that same WORD which is **ME** and the body and the water and blood that **I** took to create man that is the one **I** surrendered, so that the WORD has where to live again. The Holy Spirit, which is the SUPREME WORD, HIS home was lost.

When **I** created mankind as a house – Divine House to live in human to manage affairs as the King of Kings and the Lord of

Lords, Lucifer never wanted that. That was why Lucifer came and established that acts of politics, which is that you use money to get something that does not belong to you. He created money for manipulative usages.

Trade by barter was the natural means of exchange in that if you have soap, you use it to get say, yam. If you have plantain, you exchange it for banana. With trade by barter, if you have love and I have patience we live together. I use that ideology of exchanges for goods that is trade by barter in living life. Whatsoever you have in your life, you exchange for other things you need. The monetary aspect used for exchange came under that capacity to ease the movement of exchanges of goods.

That is what governments versus governments do in the whole world, but they use it blindly. They use it to control people and to damage a lot of things, I would have blame KING JAMES FIRST OF UNITED KINGDOM the incarnated KING SOLOMON of ISRAEL it was then this world evil politic started. As a result in a bid to get money and to rule by force you fall into what you should not, now he is KING SOLOMON ETE OF NIGERIA AFRICA.

Now, if a farmer has lots of money he would go to rule teachers. Yes, he has lots of money as a farmer and so uses his influence to lord it over a teacher, a lawyer who can never speaks the truth in his or her life, but because he has money rules over a preacher who is a master of truth and preaches the truth. With such things going on, why do you think the world will not have problems?

As **I** come to this world with the Holy Spirit to bring peace, if you as a lawyer uses your money to counter the truth you are in trouble with **ME**, not with a fellow human like you, but troubles with THE SUPREME WORD OF THE UNIVERSE, THE CREATOR. You must go back to the ordinance of God. So, today **I AM** giving the true version about the blood.

THE BLOOD IS THE **MIGHTY POWER** IN THE SYSTEM OF **MYSELF,** therefore, anybody that tells you that **THE FATHER GOD** needs blood is lying. It is Satan that needs blood. Wherever and whenever any talk arises about blood shed or sacrifices to idols and others it is evil. It has nothing to do with MY DIVINE

SELF, THE HOLY SPIRIT OF TRUTH. All evil practice they will all melt away one day, even now they are melting away one by one, In the Mighty Name and In the Mighty Blood Of Our Lord Jesus CHRIST (ENYE ODUDU ABASI MI OOO ZIM ZIM SIM ASSASSU).

Do you know what **I, THE FATHER GOD** will use to melt those things? **I AM THE SUPER SUN!** The worst thing that can happen to evil, bloodsuckers and blood drinkers is heat. They do not like heat and cannot withstand heat.
If you know that a bloodsucker or someone who is witchcraft that drinks blood whether in dream or those who drink blood lives around you, produce heat. They will melt and run away. Anybody

that has evil problems, boil water to boiling point and cover in the steam. As the heat permeates your body, it is boiling evil away. Evil is damp. They operate well in cold conditions and raining season, but when the heat comes they melt. They cannot operate well in the sun. When they go out to do evil they melt in the sun, but when darkness starts to comes they thank God.

So, the Light of God is in you. The heat in the human body is blood. That is the reason blood is very powerful. That is why evil people suck blood to survive because without blood they cannot generate their lives. That is the reason they require sacrifices. It is not God that asks for them.

Those angels that **I** drove away from Heaven use blood to survive because blood is very powerful for human life. Nonetheless, from today **I** will *search* for the blood of every person. The Supreme blood from the Supreme WORD that became flesh and died on the cross, when that blood and water dropped **I** used that to sanctify all man. That is the only holy invocation.

There is an invocation name that is authorized. Do not call the name of Angel Michael. Don't call any name, but the authorized name. Call the name of our Lord Jesus the Christ and invoke that blood – **THE POWER MIGHTY IN THE BLOOD OF OUR LORD JESUS CHRIST.** When you call that name in every situation and when that energy comes the evil energy melts and runs away. That is the reason when you call the blood of Christ, all demons, all witchcrafts melt.

THE MIGHTY POWER IN THE BLOOD OF CHRIST MELTS ALL EVIL.
Wherever you stand and say – **THE BLOOD OF OUR LORD JESUS CHRIST!** – When that blood comes that energy like hot sea, all evil melt away, because that is the SOUL of **THE SUPREME WORD**. So, you do not need to offer sacrifices again. No goat, no cow and no other human being blood as you are sinful, can produce that type of energy.

I, the Spoken Word dropped the seed of energy, the everlasting blood that **I** use to create man that is the maintenance energy for all souls for generations upon generations.

Therefore, do not kill life again and do not eat life. Do not offer sacrifices anymore. Do not call name of any angel. Call **THE FATHER GOD – OOO.** Command and invoke through the name and blood of our Lord Jesus Christ. Then **OOO** will appear. **HE** is the red blood of Christ and will sort you out. **HE** will sort the situation out for you. When you do this you escape danger of any kind.

From today, if you believe this lecture you are protected with MAXIMUM INSURANCE, MAXIMUM SECURITY and MAXIMUM PROTECTION **IN THE BLOOD OF OUR LORD CHRIST - THE BLOOD OF CHRIST!**
Christ means the KING, THE IN-CHARGE, **THE WORD** – THE SUPREME WORD OF THE UNIVERSE.

You must appreciate this **FATHER'S TALK (GOD PRESENT).**
You must appreciate this Revelation.
If you have enough money, make donation when you hear and make use of this Lecture Revelation.
Then **I** will activate **THE POWER OF THE BLOOD** in you.
Anybody that celebrates the *WORD SEASON*, also anybody that promotes the **WORD in KING SPIRITUAL LIBRARY** that is, **THE FATHER'S TALK, I** will activate the **BLOOD OF CHRIST** in you with more extra energy than before. In your mouth and in your tongue **I** will put the steel hyphen in you, so that when you say – THE BLOOD OF OUR LORD JESUS CHRIST! – Every demon bow and melts, because

that is the SUPREME ENERGY. **I call: *DESCOR CONCIUM RASTY FIAS-OUT!*** That is the title - **THE POWER MIGHTY IN THE BLOOD OF THE SUPREME WORD OF GOD – THE BLOOD OF CHRIST.**

The higher spirit of Adam, the CREATOR OF THE UNIVERSE died and shed the blood and the water to wash away all man's sins. If you commit any sin and apologize you will be forgiven. Just kneel down and pray. Call on the Christ. Invoke that holy **WORD** – the holy **BLOOD** and **WATER**, and then it will wash you clean. That is all.

That is the only *Divine Invocation* and the only blood you should use. Any other sacrifice you do you are a wanted person, because you interrupted life. Since the greater life has paid the ransom, nobody on earth should do any sacrifice again. Satan or any spirit soul or anyone should not take any bribe in the form of any sacrifice again nor should anyone offer sacrifice to Satan or any spirit soul. That is **MY** INTRODUCTION of this Lecture Revelation of today.

B: **WHAT YOU DON'T UNDERSTAND IS WHAT I WILL REVEAL TODAY**

Matter of fact with what **I** have said so far, **I** have finished the lecture. What will **I** say again? What you did not understand is what **I** have just told you. Therefore, since **I AM** the ONE that knows all things **I** will reveal things to you. The Maker knows the secret of his making and the secret of his creations. The King knows the secret of his Kingdom.

So **I** know the secrets and **I AM** telling them to you.

So, when anybody tells you come and do something because you committed sin and that you are not closer to God, assimilate this information. Nevertheless, bear in mind that the sacrifice you will do is for yourself. It is not for **ME, THE FATHER GOD.** The sacrifice of maintain the POWER OF THE BLOOD OF CHRIST in you is fasting and prayer.

Fasting is that if your conscience is not clear, because maybe, you committed fornication and fornication is waste of blood. That is why if you have sex and reduce a lot of blood in you and that blood goes into another person who is negative they will use it for evil purposes. It is not only to shed the blood in the physical that Satan uses. He collects blood also from fornication through women. Women are as small *kom-kom* (container) that is, small tank that Satan gave them to go about and collect blood – holy blood. This is for Satan to use, because he is so hungry. He cannot survive without blood. That is why you see lots of fornication everywhere. The more there is fornication, the more there are of evil practices on earth.

What brings the talk that Satan has power and demon is this or is that? It is fornication. When you go to the witchcraft world what do you do? It is fornication. They teach children how to fornicate, so that when they grow they start underage fornication.
Fornication! Fornication! Fornication! - The watchword of Satan. He is drinking blood in disguise. All the people that do these things know what **I AM**

talking about because **THE FATHER GOD** has the secret of everything in the Spiritual Record. Why do you think that Satan brought this out in this scale? Everything in television is about fornication? People keep their breasts open and go naked, all that is to entice men. All the things women do and other people do as well is to make men hungry and have lust over women, so that they continue to pump blood for Satan. Realize that the blood you are pumping is the waste of your soul. You are wasting your soul! That was what happened in Sodom and Gomorrah. When it became too much, one day fire burnt all of them down!

The more fornication that you commit and the more lies you tell as regards to any country or any place, the nearer and nearer destruction await that place. It is doom! It is darkness! Because when on one day the **WORD,** would decides on what to do with that place, you will see what takes place.

Listen carefully when you hear or see natural disasters at places know that there are serious fornication and atrocities committed in that area and the Holy Spirit destroyed that place. You will see what will happen! Therefore, if you love your country, if you love your family, if you love yourself, cut away from these practices as soon as possible, because doom awaits those who practice these things. The SUPREME SUN, which is the melting energy of the **WORD,** will arise at your door and melts all those things away and you will witness it in you. Light always drives away darkness and you cannot stand light. So that is what you do not know.

You don't know that sometimes this energy also consumes blood through eating fish and meat. There is lots of slaughtering going on. The more meat you eat is the more blood you take and it is another way of feeding evil. You collect blood and so many other things. That is the reason that those who are vegetarians – they don't eat flesh at all, Satan cannot control them because he has no link in them. That is the secret **I** reveal in this matter for you to take and guide yourself. If you have access to this Lecture, thank God and appreciate this **WORD.** What you do not know and what you do not understand is what **THE FATHER GOD** has revealed today.

Do not tell **ME** that Satan will be annoyed. Satan will not be annoyed. It is human beings that will be annoyed. It is only the agents that act for the masters. It is only agents that gangs up and go around and spy on people.

Have you seen any president go to another country to spy on them or goes to spy the enemy? No! **I** talk about what **I** do. That is why when **I** created humankind – **I AM** a portion of every living thing and every living human – so you do not need to report anybody to **ME.** That is the power of control. **I** live in everybody. Even someone that is called Satan or demon it is the **WORD** that controls that person. You can do what you do everyday, but one day **I** use **WORD** and cancel them.

Therefore, it is you that will be annoyed, because you are agent of evil. It is not Satan. Where is Satan to be annoyed in this Lecture? It is you because you are the agent. That is where you feed. Satan entered you and engineered you and you became Satan. So, when you hear what is good - when you hear positive things you became annoyed. Therefore, when destruction comes it is not Satan alone that will be destroyed, but it is also you the agent of evil! Where is Satan to be destroyed? Do you think if there was Satan to be destroyed, would **I** not have finished with him long time ago? Then everybody would rest? It is because of you! So, since **I, THE SUPREME WORD** cannot be killed and **I** will not destroy mankind, God is never destroyed. Nonetheless, you the evil person will be destroyed, because you do not respect **WORD** the in you, but **I, THE WORD** lives forever.

C: **MANY PEOPLE ARE AFRAID OF SATAN**

Agents that want to promote someone will come and say to you – ah, if you do this thing, you will see what this man will do for you. The agent will come back and say, I have told this person and he said he will carry out the assignment to kill all those people you wanted killed. The master is not the one that would go to kill. He or she will still send an agent. So, everything is down to the agent and that is what is called Satan, demon, evil and all that blah, blah, blah. They are the word, but the slip of tongues. It is your attitude. It is your mistake. It is your mind – your evil mind. You see!

People are afraid of Satan but they are not afraid of **THE FATHER GOD**, because GOD is love.
GOD is peace. God is harmony. GOD is simplicity.
GOD that is all these things is stronger than anything in the heaven and on earth, because everything exists from SUPREME SPIRIT OF ALLTHINGS-BROTHERHOOD. Even Satan says he wants to be in peace. Evil people want to be alive, because God is life, if you say to Satan or evil person die, the person will run away. The person will cry.
Don't you see that sometimes when someone commits atrocity and that Satan runs away and the person's eye open and the person would say – 'forgive me it was Satan that was directing me.' If the person is forgiven, but is not repentant, Satan goes to use that

person again. The person again says – 'forgive me, Satan was directing me.' What type of business is that? You will be destroyed with your Satan in you since you do not want to repent and follow Good part of yourself which is GOD.

When God takes glory, harmony, **HE** will take the glory with you since you followed **God** and glorified God in you. That is the meaning of you shall reap what you sow. So, if you are agent of Satan and make people afraid and turn God to be evil you will answer for that.

Some people say love means fornication while it is not so. Satan changed the word love to fornication and sex. When people have intimacy together they call it love. They use that to deceive themselves and deceive other people. All that work of evil will end through the truth.

Do not be afraid of anything. What you should be afraid of is the Spoken Word. Be afraid of God. Be afraid of the ONE who created you and who can destroy your soul if you do evil. **HE** can do anything **HE** likes to you. That is the only one you should be afraid of, from today.

Think well about this. WHO IS THE CREATOR? Bring your thought home. Consider this information. No matter who you are, if you have access to this information help **ME** to translate it into other languages of the world. So that everybody will be saved.

When you have access to this information, think this very well – WHO IS THE CREATOR?

WHO IS THE UNIVERSAL SUPREME POWER THAT EXISTS?
WHO IS ALL AND ALL?
WHO LIVES IN EVERY SOUL NO MATTER HOW LITTLE?
Conception takes seventy-two hours in the womb and after that, nine months and that spirit still alive inside the womb. That small thing inside will be born and will grow and grow and becomes a president to gives order. He will become the one that carries gun to go about killing people. He will become the one that says why don't you fear me? I can beat you up! Yet, when he was conceived by his mother did he talk like that? Was anyone afraid of him at birth? The same way you came, as foetus in the womb is the same way you will return as foetus of the earth and that is when you die. So, what

is man? What is a human being that breathes? Is it not the air of God - the Word of God that you breathe that made you call yourself human? Be careful and be clever and be wise!

Think well about this information - **WHO IS THE CREATOR?**
Who is the power?
Who is life in you?
Are you not supposed to humble yourself since you know this truth today through this information? The world was totally blind until the Holy Spirit decided to come and lead the world and expose all truth. Since you know the truth, the truth shall set you free, because the Supreme Word of Universe is now here in person talking by **HIMSELF** so that every human being will be free. God is not man but God lives in man. So, when you trouble man

you are wasting your time as God still exists because God is a Spirit. Don't see that people thought when they kill Jesus that is finished, but today Jesus Christ is the one talking now and they are the one that is finished. Oh who is Olumba Olumba Obu? The Sole Spiritual Head is ruling everywhere, but you are the one that God uses. So, every human being must obey the Spoken Word.

Jesus Christ came as the personified word to die for mankind so that when HIS **FATHER THE SPIRIT** who created the **WORD** come to the earth **HE** can now live in man. So, it has become Jehovah God and His Christ live inside human. The same thing – that spirit of truth **OOO** has come and took assumed man through Jesus Christ spirit

and born into the world. The Holy Spirit now controls the world.
That is the reason you hear this information. Yet nobody wants to know. Nevertheless, if you do not want to know you will know. The time is not yet ripe.
Think well about this information, **THE SUPREME POWER IN THE BLOOD OF THE SUPREME WORD.**

D: EVERY POWER COME FROM THE FATHER GOD

Every power came from **THE FATHER GOD.** Do you know why? Before anybody gives you instruction for anything it is via the WORD.
If the person does not say anything, that thing is not activated. All **FATHER'S TALK** has power buried by the POWER

HIMSELF and anybody that reads **THE FATHER'S TALK GOD PRESENT** becomes well if you are sick. A dead person can have life back. Any problem at all you have in this world, if you have faith and believe in **THE SUPREME WORD.** Just read **THE FATHER'S TALK GOD PRESENT** because it is the word of the Holy Spirit that surpasses every reading and every written thing. Every other written thing cannot be compared to **THE EVERLASTING GOSPEL,** is above them all. So also is **THE FATHER'S TALK GOD PRESENT** because **THE FATHER'S TALK** IS THE TESTIMONY OF EVERLASTING GOSPEL that will stay forever.

Therefore, if you have access to this, since the Holy Spirit possess

and manifests this **WORD,** this **WORD** is power itself, motivated by the **WORD** and the **SUPREME BLOOD OF CHRIST,** which is the hardware of the **WORD.**
So, if you believe in this alone, just through one page of **THE FATHER'S TALK,** all demons, all principalities, all evils melt in spirit, in soul and otherwise around you and you are free. Every power came from **THE FATHER GOD** because the **WORD** motivated everything and activates everything.

When **I** created mankind, human was just dust and a moulding Image. Then **I** breathed into man and activated man then man became a living soul. Therefore, everybody must believe that every Power Came From **THE FATHER GOD.**

Therefore, it is not something that you have to go out and struggle for – in the bush, in the water or in the air or anywhere else.

Just kneel down and speak the WORD, believe the WORD and appreciate the WORD AND THE WORD will appreciate you. You have the blood and water in you and the WORD lives in you that is the trinity GOOD-GOD. So, everything is well. When you speak negative however, the WORD will not be activated, because all negative is abusiveness of the WORD.

In contrast, when you use the WORD right – with love, with mercy, with kindness, with oneness, with righteousness, with peace – all the good things – when you use the WORD in those capacities then the **WORD** will activate **HIMSELF** and become a star in you, shinning in you and make you aware of it. You will become aware of yourself and that is the power of God in you.

Before anybody thinks anything bad the **WORD** that already lives in that person and would barrier the person. The WORD is faster. It is light. It is not a case of travelling. It is manifesting.

When **I** say to people that Light does not travel, it only manifests. For instance, when you switched on the light, it manifests instantly. Light is like life. It does not travel, it manifests instantly.

Therefore, use this as a backup understanding for your power – for the power of God to activate in you through this word. The Word of God in you is the same blood of Christ. You do not need to go get another blood or anything else. Just speak The WORD and activate that energy – the Supreme Energy of God. It is everywhere, here and there manifesting in the glory of **THE FATHER GOD**. **THE DIVINE INVOCATION IS THE NAME OF OUR LORD JESUS CHRIST**. As soon as you pronounce that name – because that body of our Lord Jesus Christ that yield the blood and that energy when you mention it, it is activated.

All glory, all power that you give to **THE FATHER GOD** – anything you want to give to THE FATHER GOD that is how you use the DIVINE INVOCATION name of God. It is **THE SUPREME NAME**. It is the greatest name. It is the name that **I, THE FATHER GOD** use to glorify **MYSELF** for eternity.

E: ELEMENTARY GODS

What is elementary god? Elementary god is negative pronouncement. Oh keep this thing here and worship it. Oh sacrifice chicken for this thing. Oh, go and bring blood; go and do this. No! Those are elementary gods.

THE FATHER GOD is the Spoken Word and elementary god is a negative pronouncement - a word that is not approved by the **SUPREME WORD OF THE UNIVERSE**. It is like particle of something. It is not the real thing, but can be used to produce a counterfeit of the real thing - a thing that has no number – a thing that is not counted with the main things. So, all those things that are not counted inclusive are nonsense. They have no meaning.

Tap power from the source. Do not therefore tap from elementary source. The **WORD** is all and all. The SPIRIT is all and all. What are you actually moulded from? What power do you infuse? You confuse the system by being negative. Therefore, the truth has now come. If you accept this truth then, all is well with you.

There should be no more elementary god. Do not worship elementary god. Do not worship anything, but believe and love everything as live and let live – as Brotherhood, but do not worship anything and do not believe anything. Just believe **THE FATHER GOD** in you – the truth that you know about God and attach your energy and your faith on that and all is well with you. And **HE** will never disappoint you.

F: GOD OUT OF GOOD SELF OF THE FATHER ALMIGHTY

It is out of good self of **THE FATHER GOD** that is why we have God. That is the meaning of God. God is out of the good self of **THE FATHER GOD. THE FATHER ALMIGHTY** has components that are good and **HE** focuses all attention to develop them. Any negativism, any bad idea, any evil idea is to be condemned and so do not promote any. That one died natural death. There is no instinct for that.

Promote instinct of goodness.
Think about good things.
Speak about good things.
Dream about all good things and not evil.
Aim for good things.
Will for good things.

When you do all that you are with **THE FATHER GOD**. Think good all the time and you are with God all the time. That good spirit, that good thoughts will manifest good spirit around you. Hear good word all the time, Speak good things and do good and then you will see the glory of God around you.

G: **I AM THE POWER OF ALL POWERS**

This power is interwoven with everything, because anything that the word created, **THE WORD** has super direct link in that thing. It is just like the fact that everybody has power, but people do not believe this power of themselves. So others use them as slaves. 'Oh come let me pray for you.' But The **WORD** lives in that person you ask to pray for. Why should someone who also has the **WORD** in them kneel down and begging for the word of other one? Can you see that?

If you remember this Lecture Revelation that equality is love, then you would know that the children that you born today, since they have the **WORD** in them, they are equal with you. It is only that that child has not grown to a certain understanding to use that WORD – to use himself or herself properly. As soon as the child can use the WORD properly, he or she is equal to you. Nonetheless, you who can use it, you are senior – senior word – senior understanding. That senior is what you use to help other WORD'S HUMAN BUILDING, but not to rule. You do not rule WORD. You do not rule God, you love GOD that WORD in every human. That is the reason there are problems all over the world.

You employ weapons and other means to try to control people. With such intention and determination you import aliens from all sorts of planets into this world because you want to rule. You use the magic and all the unnatural things they brought and all of them to back you up to rule people. You are in trouble. You will be debased because all these people you suppress are Gods and they will fight against you spiritually. That is how the WORD fights against people.
All the people that are well known when they misuse their position they eventually become poor. They become wanted persons. That is what happens because you use position to suppress other Gods. Then you are in trouble.

Every Spoken Word is God. Every spirit that lives in every man is God. But **THE FATHER GOD ALMIGHTY** surpasses all. When you stand on the side of positive then, negative is destroyed in your presence.

CONCLUSION A: **ALL THE POWERS IN HEAVEN AND ON EARTH ARE WITH THE CHRIST OF THE FATHER GOD ALMIGHTY**

THE FATHER GOD ALMIGHTY IS THE SPIRIT ALMIGHTY. The Christ of **THE FATHER GOD ALMIGHTY** is the Supreme WORD of the universe - The **WORD** that became the Living Soul and manifested as human being. Everything manifested through the

WORD. Everything is done through the WORD. So you can see that the **WORD** is King of kings and the Lord of the Lords. But this King of Kings and the Lord of Lords resides in man. That is, man is the House of God. When you say you are going to church or that you are going to the House of God, you are going to see human beings there. If you get there and you did not see any human being knows then that you did not see God there. That is what is happening. That is the truth about the whole matter.

So, if you worship one supreme man – one senior human being who is the King of Kings and the Lord of Lords who is your Father Adam then you are worshipping **GOD THE FATHER.** If you respect and appreciate the **WORD** then, you appreciate God. If you appreciate the **SUPREME SPIRIT** that made everything then you appreciate **THE FATHER GOD ALMIGHTY.** That is exactly what it is.

Spirit is **THE FATHER GOD ALMIGHTY.** The **WORD** is God and that **WORD** that lives in man made man becomes **God The Father.**

CONCLUSION B: **THE SUPREME WORD IS EVERYTHING**

When that Supreme Word is motivated in man it becomes everything. That is why you see all the things that are managed and done in the world and man become chief administrator and everything. In a nutshell you are serving the WORD and the WORD is serving you also. So, you and the WORD are one including the SPIRIT, which altogether equals one – the trinity, just as in life the spirit, the blood and water are one and make you a whole living human being. Any day your body is short of any of the three components then, you no longer exist physically. The **WORD** will find its way. The BLOOD will find its way and the WATER also finds its way, then you have finished here.

CONCLUSION *C:* **THE POWER MIGHTY IN THE BLOOD OF THE SUPREME WORD OF THE UNIVERSE (CHRIST)**

This is where this lecture came about – **THE POWER MIGHTY IN THE BLOOD.** The blood of the **WORD** is the Christ of God –

the blood of the King of Kings and the Lord of Lords – the blood of God. So you do not need another blood.

If you sacrifice anything else you are a coward. You are a stubborn person. You do not believe **THIS WORD**. If you believe just connect yourself to it. It does not cost you anything to believe. What it will cost you is the faith. Just believe this information and you are already initiated in Christ, your original Father Adam's Supreme Soul.

You don't need to initiate into anything in this world. Lots of people have tested and have seen that **God HIMSELF IS THE POWER OF THE BLOOD OF CHRIST.** So, just call that name when you know that negative spirit is around you. Just believe in the Spoken Word. Pray and say –

ALL IS WELL. **THE FATHER** HAS CONQUERED. That is the power in the word. When you speak like that all atmosphere clears and the light of God, which is the Holy Spirit, will come and melts out evil. Evil cannot stand that Light. That is the sort of Spirit I take and barrier all principalities not to go near to the children of God, now and forever more. Amen.

LET MY PEACE AND BLESSINGS ABIDE WITH ALL THE PEOPLE WITH INSTANT REACTION OF ACCEPTANCE WHEN YOU MENTION THE SUPREME MIGHTY BLOOD OF CHRIST, THE BLOOD OF THE SUPREME WORD THAT I ACTIVATED FOREVER TO SALVAGE ALL THE CHILDREN OF GOD IN THE

ENTIRE WORLD, NOW AND FOREVER MORE. AMEN.
THANK YOU FATHER!
THANK YOU FATHER!
THANK YOU FATHER!

THANK YOU FATHER

CHAPTER TWO

THE SUPREME ALTAR

FATHER'S TALK
(GOD PRESENT)
Christ our Lord, Sixteenth Simon Canaanite, FATHER Two Thousand and Eight (AF.OB.BOOH)
(Saturday, Sixteenth February, Year Two Thousand and Eight (16.02.2008))

In the Name of Our Lord Jesus Christ, In the Blood of Our Lord Jesus Christ, Now and Forever more

THE SUPREME ALTAR
===================

Today! It pleases **ME, THE FATHER GOD THE CREATOR OF THE UNIVERSE** to give this Lecture Revelation. The Lecture Revelation of today is titled: **THE SUPREME ALTAR.**

INTRODUCTION

I advise all hearts and all souls that have the opportunity to come into contact or have any sort of access to **THE FATHER'S TALK (GOD PRESENT)** Lectures Revelation, to be humble in their heart and in their spirit when reading or listening to any of these Revelation Lectures.

As you know, the Spoken Word that lives in human being is God but **THE SUPREME WORD OF THE UNIVERSE, FROM THE SUPREME THOUGHT OF THE FATHER GOD IS THE FATHER HIMSELF.**

The **WORD** is everything and the **WORD** lives in you and that **WORD** is the LIFE of the World. Therefore, this **WORD** that you are hearing now, in whatsoever form is not a mere **WORD**. It is not a **WORD** that came from any individual of a human being.

THIS WORD IS FROM ME, THE SUPREME WORD OF THE UNIVERSE, HE IS THE FATHER – THE FATHER GOD ALMIGHTY.

I AM therefore, inviting your soul and your spirit to take the good directions in humility, oneness of spirit and positivity as well as to possess the spirit of calmness. When you have a humble heart a peaceful mind, then you can listen to or read **THE FATHER'S TALK (GOD PRESENT)** without arrogance. **I** have rebuked all negativism, all evils in you and the entire world.

As **I AM** giving this Lecture Revelation Information all principalities, all instincts, all emotions and everything else that do not bring glory to **THE**

FATHER GOD that affected your mind, your heart and your actions are sent away, through **MY Supreme Light of the HOLY SPIRIT**.

THE SUPREME WORD manifests the **Supreme Light**. All the vicinity that this WORD is heard as well as wherever this WORD is found is captured by the **Supreme Light of THE FATHER GOD**.

The Light of God drives away all evil. You will then be left clean and clear to listen to this WORD, so that this WORD should save your soul.

A: **WHAT IS THE MEANING OF ALTAR**

I know people talks about **Altar** with varied meanings according to individual perceptions.

What Is The Meaning of Altar?

Altar can mean so many things.
Altar in a given context can mean something for or a place of sacrifice.
Altar can be a Shrine.
Altar can be a Temple.
Altar can also mean a private place or a secret place.
Altar can mean a sacred place, a holy place.
Altar can mean whatsoever you term altar to be.

Altar in the human sense is where you seclude a place, set it up and revere it.
Altar in the spiritual sense means, where valuables are kept.

Bank is an **Altar** for money.
A woman is an **Altar** for a man.
A man is an **Altar** of the Spirit, either Holy Spirit or elementary spirit.

A package, a carton, a container all means **Altar.**

The question now is: who alters **Altar?**

THE SUPREME ALTAR that alters the **Altar** is **THE SUPREME WORD. I, THE SPIRIT** alters the WORD and the WORD alters man and then creations take place. Creations manifest through the WORD. Without the WORD nothing would have come to existence in the physical reality.

In the beginning was the WORD and the WORD was with God and God was with man. That God that the WORD manifested from has manifested through man on earth. This world as a whole is an **Altar** of the SPIRIT.

This world as a whole is the premises of **THE FATHER GOD.**

This world is the **ALTAR OF THE FATHER GOD ALMIGHTY. I** have to reveal that the Supreme Premises of **THE FATHER GOD** is this world. That is the reason there is no space that anybody or any spirit object soul can claim to own. None can say, "I own this, I own that." Making such claim is fighting against **THE FATHER GOD.** Some people call themselves President, a King, a Queen, a great person, Army man, this and that and take the laws into their hands. Such persons are just destroying their soul because everyone is only a creation of **THE FATHER GOD, THE SUPREME ALTAR.**
THIS WORLD AS A WHOLE IS A PREMISES OF **THE FATHER GOD.**

I, THE FATHER GOD created the world and the whole universe as **MY** premises. I established the different nations, several diverse homes as well as created all the many different planets. So, all the various things that live in the world are living in the premises of God.

I AM THE SUPREME ALTER. I ALTER things every second and I control everything. I live in everything. There is no single creation that I do not have access into. **I AM THE ONLY SPIRIT THAT CAN ALTER THE ALTAR.** So, **What Is The Meaning of Altar?**
Use this Lecture Revelation of today to guide yourself to know how you move on this earth because it is good for you to

understand things so that you know how to treat things.

It happens that a lot of people know certain things, but they hide it from other people. Some elementary forces and elementary human beings use craftiness to trick people to do what they are not supposed to do. Today, you will know why problems entered into the world and the different ways you can escape these problems. **What Is The Meaning of Altar?**

You are the **Altar.** Every human soul physically is the **Altar**.
SPIRIT **ALTAR** the soul,
The soul **ALTAR** human,
Human **ALTAR** things in action on earth, with this understanding and with this super wisdom; you will know how to behave. You will know how to treat yourself

and how to treat others as well as how to **THINK WELL** because if you **THINK WELL, SPEAK WELL** and **HEAR WELL** then you will **ACT WELL**. It then means you are behaving well in the premises of **THE FATHER GOD**, which is yourself.

Human being is Heaven and Earth as far as man and woman are concerned. Where did **I** keep man after **I** created man? Man lives in spirit, in soul and in the physical reality.

When you are not living here physically on earth, where are you? You are in the soul. And when you are in the soul you are also in spirit. That spirit is **THE FATHER GOD HIMSELF.** That soul however, is an object creation. That means at the activation of your name you are now created as an object idea that existed before manifestation.

Any idea is an object soul and must always manifest from time to time. That is why people have to believe incarnation and reincarnation.

Prior to nature bringing you out, you did not exist. Therefore, incarnation and reincarnation would not feature in such circumstance.

When the **WORD** manifest an object soul and give it a name, say Adam and Eve, Abel and Lith, Cain and Sudia and or Seth, that object soul will continue to exist. It can never ever cease to exist because **I THE SUPREME WORD THE SPIRIT OF ALL THINGS** created them and the lives in them when they become humans. The object souls become human beings and live on earth.

When any human being is no more that object soul, that idea still exists. That being the case from time to time **THE SUPREME ALTAR** who is **THE SUPREME NATURE** that **Altar** will bring the object soul back on earth to form yet again physical objects. That is what is known as manifestation and that yields incarnation and reincarnation in subsequent manifestations.

The SUPREME SPIRIT **Altar** the **WORD** and The **WORD Altar** ideas and creates the ideas through speaking the WORD. The WORD creates and manifests ideas and brings into notice what nobody knew. What nobody heard the SPIRIT will bring it into notice via the WORD and people would start to hear of such idea and then know and marvel at the creation and say, "Oh this is the thing!"

When a woman is pregnant, no one knows whether it is a baby boy or a baby girl that she will put to birth. During pregnancy the gender of the foetus is not known unless of course a pregnancy scan is carried out to reveal whether the baby is boy or a girl. That is the physical side.

When the child is actually born and given a name that became an idea with a physical object. That object idea has become man or woman that is, human being. With that even if the child lived for just one second and goes back, an object soul has been formed and so the child can always come back as human being.

The child is able to come back because he or she has a soul object that cannot die. That is the meaning of **Altar.**

THE SUPREME ALTAR is the SPIRIT that has effect in every situation. **HE** is the cause and effect of every matter.

B: WHO ALTAR WHO

This is the big question. **Who Altar Who?**
I want to use this Lecture Revelation to train all positive humans particularly those who are positive, although they do not know that they are in elementary stage of their lives, which made them behave as negatives. Also sometimes they do not know what they are doing.

This Revelation Lecture does not need interpretation. Just read and activate the Spirit of **THE FATHER GOD** in you by believing it. Then **THE FATHER GOD** who is the ONE that is giving this information will be the ONE to be in your heart to analyse things properly for you.

THIS REVELATION LECTURE IS FROM **THE SUPREME SPIRIT OF THE FATHER GOD.** Read it with that knowledge and understanding. If you are reading this WORD, which is from **THE SUPREME SPIRIT OF THE FATHER GOD** as a Revelation Lecture, while you are reading it, being that **I, THE SUPREME WORD** giving you this Lecture Revelation, you will not need interpretation because inside your heart **I** will have activated **MYSELF** in you while you are reading it. The same thing is applicable if you are listening to it. **I, THE FATHER GOD** will activate **MYSELF** in you and you will understand more because **I**

AM now INPUT and OUTPUT in you. That is to say that this information will become the input that output the whole scenario of you, which is the whole system of yourself. So, just activate **ME, THE FATHER GOD** in your heart by believing this Revelation Lecture and by having humility inside you.

If you believe that this WORD is not a human word but The WORD from **THE SUPREME WORD, THE FATHER GOD ALMIGHTY** that means you have activated **ME** in your heart. When you have **ME** in your heart, **I** will immediately analyse everything you do not understand and you will then have full understanding about that issue. As **I Altar** you, **I** will immediately explain things by **MYSELF** inside of you as the Supreme Thought.

All that you need to do is to be positive and not negative.
All that you need to do is to have love and have humility.
All that you need to do is to have oneness spirit.
All that you need to do is to forgive one another.

If someone offends you, do not carry the feelings of hurt and resentment about with you for more than twenty-four hours. Forgive the person who offended you. You need to become simple. You should allow the happiness and the flavour of joy of **THE FATHER GOD** to swim around your heart.

Make your environment and your vicinity to be clean. Then **I, THE SUPREME ALTAR** will **altar** you and activate your system and your heart.

I AM living in your heart and from your heart **I** will take control of your entire system.

I will become the light that is shining over your soul and your heart. You will see that the system of your soul will become light. When **I AM** in you and **Altar** you there will be a sign that The Supreme Holy Spirit of God is in you. Any house that **THE FATHER GOD Altar** there is a difference in that house. So, why not allow **THE FATHER GOD** to **Altar** you all the time so that YOU CAN **ALTAR THE FATHER GOD** instead of allowing all manners of evil, elementary forces and unnecessary thoughts to over-shadow you. This is the only way that you would know **Who Altar Who.**

Allow **THE SUPREME GOD - THE FATHER GOD**

ALMIGHTY to be in you. First of all confess your sins. If you know that you fornicate, you commit adultery, you tell lies and you do all sorts of bad things, just put yourself in **The Maintenance System of The Holy Spirit**.

What is **The Maintenance System of The Spirit** of **THE FATHER GOD?**

The **Maintenance System of The Positive Spirit** are fasting and prayer and confessions of sins. It means you apologise in your heart for your sins. If the sin you committed is too much just find someone you know to be positive and let the person be a witness physically that you have confessed that sin. Thereafter, your conscience is clear of that sin you committed. Or if you committed the sin against someone, if it is possible, go to that person you committed the sin against and make the confession. Let your conscience be clear.

As soon as your conscience is clear, you have cleaned your environment. You have sent all the evils away. There are no more maggots and bad odour around you. As your environment is clean, you can then invite **The Supreme Nature – The Supreme Spirit – the Holy Spirit** into you.

The **Holy Spirit** however, will automatically come when you sweep the house clean. The **Holy Spirit** will come through you reading the Holy writ. You can: Read positive portions of the Bible, Read **THE EVERLASTING GOSPEL.** Read **FATHER'S TALK (GOD PRESENT)** Lectures Revelations. You can read any words that are positive in order to maintain that environment for **The Holy Spirit, The Supreme Nature** who is **THE FATHER GOD ALMIGHTY** to come into you. That is the way to activate Christ, the King of Kings and the Lord of Lords who is the **SUPREME WORD** in you. That means you have now **Altar ME, THE FATHER GOD.** Then **I, THE SUPREME FATHER GOD,** will **Altar** you.

As soon as **I** come into you, your situation will change for good. You will become a changed person, a rearranged human being in a positive way.

This also happens to those who invite evil in them. In their case they change in a negative way.

I, THE FATHER GOD coming into you is the only way you can drive away demons around and inside you. That is the only way you can drive away evils in and around you. That is the only way you can drive away spirits of witchcraft and wizard inside you and around you.

If you happen to suspect that some kind of negative influence is around you that is to say that a foreign spirit that is not supposed to live in you is in you, invite **ME, THE FATHER GOD ALMIGHTY** to come into you because **I** created mankind as **MY OWN** home to live in, but Satan, the evil spirit soul squats in some human of **MY** home. The evil spirits on earth are the frustrated souls, the negative spirits, spirit of mammon, the spirit of those who look for money in a bad way. All are Satan, the negative spirit that roam about everywhere in the world looking for where to live.

Do not forget that **I, THE SUPREME FATHER GOD ALMIGHTY, THE HOLY SPIRIT OF TRUTH** alone own mankind. **I** created human being and live in human. **I** also created all living creatures and also live in them, but the frustrated evil spirits souls are not welcome back into **MY** Divine Self. The negative words, the negative actions and the negative souls form evil all over the place.

People tell lies; people kill and people commit all sorts of sins. They have annoyance in them. They fight and kill and they curse. All those evil cannot come back to **ME** as **THE HOLY SUPREME WORD**. So, they hang around and live as *Parasitingsite*. They are called *flashing-pass by*. They are evil spirits souls.

Those negative spirits souls can live in you and influence you and **Altar** you. When they enter into you, your situation changes for evil, at first you will not be happy. You emotions will change. You will have bad mind. It will yield so many evil and bad minds around you. It can turn good things to be evil because the environment has gone bad.

Let **ME** use this analogy to demonstrate a situational change. If say you board a public transport and are travelling to somewhere on a bright sunny beautiful day and on the way the sun does not shine anymore. Before you knew it thick dark cloud has covered the sky. Then it started to rain very heavily. As a result the warm weather changed so dramatically to become chilly. What is the effect then?

The condition of the whole place has changed. You, probably along with others will start feeling cold. If people were chatty and bubbly and bright, they would go quiet. Some could become sullen and grumpy because the condition of the whole place has changed. At other places people would run for shelter from the rain. They are likely to fold their arms and look gloomy while waiting for the rain to subside or stop. That is how the sign of evil is. Bad weather is an example of evil.

When you surrender yourself to bad thinking and you cannot rebuke it, your mood changes. **I** gave a Lecture Revelation called ***THE BUTTON OF HOLD*** and also ***ADVANCED AND PROGRESSING MIND.*** All the Lectures are to train every human being and to bring you man into

perfection, so that you will know how to maintain **the Holy Spirit, the Supreme WORD** in you and have everlasting life with perfect **PEACE**.
You can live as long as you like. You can live without sickness. You can live in this world and do better things if you listen to the **POSITIVE WORDS OF THE FATHER GOD**.

Who Altar Who means that as you allow the Holy Spirit of God into you and you activate the positive self of **THE FATHER GOD** in you and your environment is clean. Then **I, THE SUPREME WORD** will **Altar** you.
If, for instance you are expecting a visitor, you tidy your home. You arrange the chairs properly, dust the house and generally clean the house because of the visitor or

visitors you are expecting in your home. Similarly if you invite **ME, THE POSITIVE SPIRIT OF THE FATHER GOD**, there are ways you will have to conduct yourself, your heart, your body and everything about you so that your invitation will be honoured. Also note that there are ways you would conduct yourself and your invitation will not be honoured. For instance, supposed you look nice, but you argue, you fornicate, you tell lies and do all sorts of other bad things. You eat fish as well as meat. Eating those flesh have bad effect in you even though partial, but particularly they drive away the Holy Presence of **THE FATHER GOD** in you. What you eat can affect you and your system. For instance, when someone eats certain food and breaks wind afterwards, the smell

can be very unpleasant because of the nature of the food you ate. People would not like to be around you because of the awful odour from you when you break wind from your behind. It is the same thing with what is in you.
Whatever it is that **Altar** you affect you physically spiritually and otherwise affect you.
What you eat affects your system. What affects your system affects your soul.
What affects your soul affects **The Holy Spirit** around you. All work together.

These physical analogies demonstrate the discomfort of **The Holy Spirit of truth** to runaway from living in you.
Let's say you found human waste that is, faeces with unbearable stench lodged and scattered all over your bed. You would not lie

on that bed like that. You would clean it up thoroughly and replace the sheets and all the beddings for your bed to be nice and clean again to lie on.

Or let's say as it turned out the faeces were not just on the bed alone but equally flung all over the floors and walls of your house and with such rancid smell. You cannot stay in that house like that. You would clean your house wall to wall including the floors. Then you could decide to disinfect and sanitize the house through and through before staying there again. Even if it were just at your front door that someone left a lump of putrid human waste, you would not feel comfortable passing through it into your house. You would get rid of it properly and wash your front entrance to comfortably enter your house.

That is the situation of **The Holy Spirit of Truth** with humans involved with evil activities. Also when you have a bath and wear clean fresh cloths you feel refreshed and comfortable. When you clean your mouth, you feel very refreshed too and would enjoy your food better. You are comfortable when everything is clean around you. The same thing applies to the **Supreme Holy Spirit of Truth**, THE FATHER GOD ALMIGHTY. When your environment is clean **HE** is comfortable to live in you.

People call God! God! God! They could be calling evil for all their shouting of God. You can call **THE FATHER GOD, THE HOLY SPIRIT** but it is not the one that you called that came to you. Are you giving out invitation indirectly to the negative spirit when you purport to call **THE FATHER GOD?**

Suppose you called **THE FATHER GOD** but you became annoyed, you engaged in all sorts of bad things, you drink blood and practice all sorts of evil, you are wicked to people. What you have automatically and indirectly invited is evil. When you think evil you have invited evil. When you speak evil you have invited evil.

If you think good thoughts you have invited goodness into you. If you speak good words you have invited goodness into you. If your practical actions are positive, you have invited positive presence. That is, you have invited the Positive Presence of **THE FATHER GOD** into you. That is the good atmosphere. That is how to **ALTAR** the **ALTAR** and the **ALTAR ALTAR ALTAR.**

C: **THE SUPREME HOLY SPIRIT NEEDS YOU AS A HOME**

I know some people will not take this Revelation Lecture kindly. Nevertheless, there are many people now on earth who come from the inspiration of the positive spirit of **THE FATHER GOD.** They will be so happy and overwhelmed with joy and excitement to hear this message.

There are clever human beings on earth who do not ask such question as, "Who cooked the food?" Or when they go to buy cloth in the market would first of all want to know who sewed the cloth. So long as you see that the material is good, the design is trendy and the pattern is fine, you buy the cloth and wear it. On the other side those who made the cloth just wanted their money. Those who sell food in the shop do not care who buys their food. All they know is that they want to sell their food.

As it does not matter that when you go to eat in a restaurant, you do not particularly care who cooked the food. Also, when you go to the bank to get some money you do not know who paid in the money that the bank took to pay you. Or even to get money from cash points, you don't know the immediate source of the money at the cash point from which you made a withdrawal. The commercial banks do not print the money. The money could have travelled to everywhere and back before coming into the bank. So,

why do you question where this WORD came from? 'Who speaks this WORD?
Who gives these instructions?
Who wrote this?
Who published this?'

Does it matter who did all those? What matters is -This WORD, is it true?
Does it sound well?
Is it positive WORD?
Does it have any meaning?
If what you are hearing or reading so far has any meaning to your ears, being that it is positive WORD, then you will appreciate it. Unless you are negative then you won't like the information contained here. If you are positive then you will hate negative things. By their fruits ye shall know them.

Many people call God, God, God just with their lips alone! They

only pretend to worship **THE FATHER GOD.** There are also those who pretend to be good.
I will know all of them according to how they accept this GOOD information.
I will know them according to how overwhelming their joy and support of the entire **FATHER'S TALK (GOD PRESENT)** Revelation Lectures are.

I, THE FATHER GOD ALMIGHTY, THE CREATOR OF THE UNIVERSE is broadcasting this information via the mouth of HRM King Solomon ETE. Therefore, HRM King Solomon David Jesse ETE is not the person talking here per se. This is just as your television air information to you from the Television Broadcasting Station. Or the Radio Station broadcasting information and you receive it from your radios at home. Consequently, **I, THE FATHER GOD, I AM THE STATION MYSELF. I AM THE BROADCASTER. I AM THE ONE TALKING-TALKING THIS FATHER'S TALK (GOD PRESENT). THIS IS DIRECT FROM THE FATHER GOD – 'AFTER THOSE DAYS SAYS THE LORD MOST HIGH.'**

You cannot bury the Truth. The TRUTH has come out by **HIMSELF** now. If you know the Truth, the Truth shall set you free. Remember that **The Supreme Holy Spirit of Truth** needs you as a home to live in you.

Even as you are hearing this WORD, if your heart is clean and if you are positive and this WORD **Altar** you and stay in you, it will then be possible for you to extend this information to others. You can obtain extra copies of this information and promote it because you know that it is true. Bear in mind that no evil mind or negative mind will ever promote positive words or positive programs for that matter.

All the programes that **I, THE FATHER GOD, THE SUPREME WORD OF CREATION** established by **MYSELF** through HRM King Solomon David Jesse ETE are positive and so are permanent, everything **I** do through Him is positive.

Do not look at HRM King Solomon David Jesse ETE on himself as human. You should rather look at the truth. **MY INDWELLING SPIRIT** IN HRM KING SOLOMON DAVID

JESSE ETE IS THE MANIFESTATION OF THE FOLLOWING PROGRAMS:
THE **SUPREME WORD**
SEASONAL CELEBRATION
THE TRINITY CELEBRATION
THE FATHER'S TALK (GOD PRESENT)
THE SONGS OF DAVID SOLOMON,
THE SPIRITUAL HOSPITAL - that He uses only Spoken Word to witness the healing.

So, all these good things are what you want to call Satan. You want to call them evil. You want to call them negative. Are those how negative operates? Is that how you are supposed to think about positive things? By their fruits ye shall know them.

THE ARK OF THE NEW COVENANT is POSTERITY as the WORD Centre. The Ark of the

New Covenant, which is LOVE! LOVE! LOVE! - is also to posterized **MY** WORD by King Solomon David Jesse ETE. So, check all these programmes well.

You want to condemn Him as soon as you hear His name and also when you hear this WORD. Do you have any access to see and hear Him? If you do not have access to see and hear Him in person, have access to **THE FATHER'S TALK (GOD PRESENT) in King Solomon Spiritual Library, The Information of THE FATHER GOD**. That is all you need.
You don't even need to see Him. You don't need to worry about Him. Just take the information and pass on the information to all and sundry if you are positive. Pass on this positive information to everybody on earth then, the world

shall change for good. Then **The Holy Spirit of Truth** wills **Altar** every heart that prepared their selves and that made themselves holy sanctuaries of **THE FATHER GOD.**

You don't need ceremony to make yourself the **Altar** of **THE FATHER GOD.** If you believe this information and forgive one another, if you have love and mind your own business lives and let lives life, you have made yourself the **Altar of THE FATHER GOD.** Think well, speak well, hear well and do well.

Do not listen to things that are not good.

Do not attach importance to things that are not good. Build a fence around yourself with things that are positive. Send all negatives away. Do not allow them to come close to you.

When you do this in your heart and in your soul, then all negative evils will stand at the back door and outside the gate. They will not reach you. With this practice you will be able to keep yourself with the Holy Spirit and **I, THE FATHER GOD** will live in you as **the Supreme WORD, the Positive Holy Spirit of Truth** that will manifest everything good. Thereafter, your environment must surely be good. If it does not work today, it must surely work tomorrow.

All those who are positively inclined in their heart, their environments and their future starting from now will be all positive and things are going to be good.

No evil can overcome goodness.

No Satan can come closer to light because truth means light of the world.

Since you now understand that **I, THE SUPREME HOLY SPIRIT TRUTH,** need you as a home and to become **MY Altar,** then set your mind to achieve the good environment for **ME** to occupy you. You do not need any ceremony. You do not need to offer any sacrifices. All that you need to do is to use your heart to accept this **WORD,** this **DIVINE INFORMATION** and all is well with you, In the Name and blood of Our Lord Jesus Christ.

D: WHAT HAPPENED TO ADAM AND EVE

What Happened To Adam And Eve? Do you ask yourself that question?

What happened with Adam and Eve was that after **I, THE FATHER GOD** created Adam and Eve as **MY** Home **I** put them in **MY** premises, which is this world - Africa to be precise, then the evil one came and deceived them.

When you read the Lecture Revelation titled: *NIGERIA IN AFRICA* you will know how **I** started the creation of the world on this earth. You will also know how **I** manifested **MYSELF** for the first time as the Spoken Word.

I created Adam and Eve as male and female to represent Heaven and Earth. They also represent the Father and the Mother, the son and the daughter, the husband and the wife. All of them mean one thing. When the two come together they become one. When the two are separated they become supporter for each other. The evil heart - the negative self - the premature self however, went and deceived them. That was what happened to them. Instead of them to be perfect **Altar** of **THE FATHER GOD** they became **altar** of the infidel spirit - Satan.

That was how human-animals came about. **I** created four living creatures' animals, birds, fish and mankind. Man was the only human being who was Adam and then Eve. At the fall of Adam and Eve however, the three living creatures had access to develop themselves as humans. Lucifer used the serpent to deceived Eve and corrupted her. Eve in turn passed the virus on to Adam. The result of animal infected Adam and Eve became the various human-animals that parade the earth as real human beings.

Adam and Eve would have continued to be positive man and positive woman. They would have had children who would have been all positive male and positive female. That was **MY** plan of the **Positive Altar** and of the Tree of Life and Death.

What took place was that in the Garden of Eden animals could not speak. They could not and still do not speak or make any meaningful utterances. There were no creations that could speak apart from **THE FATHER GOD'S** creations Adam and Eve, who were the human beings. At that time there was no evil on earth. Man was the **Altar** of the positive Supreme WORD, while other creations including animals, birds and fish and all others were angels and servants to man. When Adam and Eve became corrupted events began to unfold. The serpent being an animal that could not speak the WORD to form any creations was able to speak.

How that came to be was that Lucifer, the enemy of **THE FATHER GOD** – the other self – the negative self of **THE FATHER GOD** decided to have a Queendom as the female part. She wanted to establish her own domain, instead of sharing with **THE FATHER GOD.** When Lucifer was sent out of Heaven down to earth, she needed to gain access back into Adam to be able to establish her Queendom. But she could not have access to Adam and also no access to Eve on earth because **I, THE FATHER GOD** put up a barrier to guard against that happening. She however, had access to the animals and the serpent became a willing tool to perpetrate her negative plan. Lucifer, the negative self therefore, used the animal instincts, which included cunning and craftiness gain access into Adam. As the negative self she was able to put herself into a lower creation, the serpent. Then the serpent changed and started to talk. When the serpent changed and started to talk, it went and talked to Eve.

The animal said to Eve, you see, **THE FATHER GOD** said you should not eat that fruit in the Garden of Eden. That is because when you eat it your eyes will open. Eve was surprised to hear an animal spoke for the first time. This talk however, was not a physical dialogue but all were done in spirit soul.

Adam and Eve were spirits. They were pure spirits. They were Gods. They could understand animal instincts. They could understand and hear the animals but the animals could not understand them.

Adam and Eve could manipulate things, but that was the first time Eve clearly heard a serpent spoke. That deceived Eve's heart.

The serpent brought beautiful things to the attention of Eve. First of all 'he' made Eve understood she was very beautiful. He made Eve to go and see herself on the water by using the water as mirror. She looked and saw her reflection on the water and admired herself. And she saw that she was beautiful.

Then the serpent said to her, don't you see you are naked? Go and cover yourself. He showed Eve a lot of things including sexual instincts and other knowledge of negativism. Eve then had the awareness that she was naked.

What was the meaning of that action?
Lucifer **Altar** the serpent and also **Altar** Eve, the same Lucifer inside the serpent was the same Lucifer inside Eve. The same Lucifer looked for a way to enter into Adam. That is how witchcrafts and wizards operate.

When Lucifer passed the negative instincts to Eve, Eve then looked for a way to be inside Adam. As soon as Eve had fornication with Adam and kissed Adam she vomited the whole things into Adam. The result became that a foreign spirit **Altar** Adam who was the House of **THE FATHER**

GOD and lived in the premises of **THE FATHER GOD.**

I was not pleased with what happened, but **I** did not destroy Adam and Eve because if **I** had destroyed them that day, **I** would have destroyed **MY** house final.

Being that **I AM** LOVE, **I** used love on the whole situation. Immediately **I** called **MY** Positive Throne of Love to have mercy. Then **I** persuaded Satan to go into kneeling position and **I** subdued her. Then **I** reduced serpent into eating dust. **I** took away the serpent's legs and reduce the animal to crawling in the dust. Then **I** sent Lucifer to be wandering about. She became the confusing spirit soul that goes about deceiving people.

The wandering spirit soul called Satan or Lucifer or whatsoever, is a frustrated spirit self and the one that is always looking for where to live.

The aim of Satan's actions was to make **ME, THE FATHER GOD** the wanderer and to become frustrated. For she knew that as she had entered into Adam and Eve, **I, THE FATHER GOD** had nowhere to live again in full capacity has personified **SUPREME WORD**, **I** couldn't live in animal. She actually temporary succeeded.

Then **I** went away from Adam and Eve and as a result **I** sent them out of **MY** premises, outside the Gate of the Garden of Eden. Do not forget that the whole world belongs to **ME THE FATHER GOD,** but **I** sent them away from **MY** presence.

That action was that they would not behold **THE FATHER GOD'S** presence again. They had become animal presence. They had negative part inside of them. From since that time of Adam and Eve incident human beings became polluted.

Human kind became polluted because another thing has **Altar** man. So the **Holy Altar** became evil altar, managed by the negative spirit soul.

The first thing **I** did after the incident was to send Adam to fast. **I** used to hide Adam. The reason **I** sent them away from the Garden of Eden was so that they would not see any food most of the time. That left them with no option than to go without food and so that became fasting for them.

I created Eve in the nature of Lucifer, the female part. So, she had to do with the physical food, carnal things, the mundane world and fanciful things. When Lucifer therefore, took over Eve she started to bring out the idea of fanciful things, carnal things and enjoyment of the physical life. Lucifer showed Eve all the knowledge of this world. When Cain was born, he represented the physical aspects of things and carnality in all its forms.

The spirit of witchcraft is the spirit soul that is used to create things in the mundane world. This witchcraft spirit soul can be used to create positive things as well as negative things. Witchcraft however, is a carnal thing called in spirit HYIE' KA'KE. It is of the mundane world. Some people use the spirit of witchcraft to create the mundane Queendom. They create their Queendom in this world filled with beautiful things, which they use witchcraft to obtain. Witchcraft is also used to kill and destroy. That is the reason that everything mundane is perishable. They need energy to survive.

Majority of people use witchcraft, which is evil spirit soul to create their wealth. These evil spirits require blood to fuel for their negative energy. All the people that are into witchcraft know what **I AM** talking about.

When you talk about the acquisition of money, money takes blood. A lot of blood is shed to acquire money. When you talk about the mundane world, at the root of it, it has to do with blood. That is because they do not live through the positive energy. They live through the negative energy. All rituals are caused by the mundane Queendom of the world.

The idea of the blood of Christ was for **THE FATHER GOD ALMIGHTY** to capture the mundane world. It was that Adam would come again and would die. After His death, the mundane world would then become that of THE FATHER GOD and all the practices would become positive. There would be no rituals and uses of negative energy to maintain anything again in the world, so witchcraft spirit soul is melted and die. Adam came back as JESUS CHRIST meaning KING OF KINGS and LORD OF LORDS. The Supreme blood of Adam as the God the Father of human race, who came as Our Lord Jesus Christ took care of that situation. Therefore, you do not need any ritual to obtain money. You do not need to shed any blood to have money. Satan nonetheless, still parades the old idea and people still fall victim to that. He still convinced people that until you made some sort of evil sacrifice, you would not have money. That is NOT true. The **ALTAR OF THE FATHER GOD, THE HOLY SPIRIT OF TRUTH** is here to back you up and give you the energy to survive, to live on earth and be rich without offering any evil sacrifices, without rituals and shedding blood whatsoever. So, that was what happened with Adam and Eve in the Garden of Eden and the reason they gave birth to Cain who continued evil on earth, and also why they gave birth to Abel who continued the positive procreation on earth. **I** have said these things in so many **FATHER'S TALK (GOD PRESENT)** lectures revelations and so everybody should know the whole true story by now.

E: **YOUR POSITIVE AND NEGATIVE SELF IS INSIDE OR OUTSIDE OF YOU**

This is a very important point. At that time when the evil spirit soul **Altar** Adam and Eve every human being became infected so **I** sent everyone away from **MY** presence. But now in this world you can live in **MY** premises or you can live outside **MY** premises.

If you are negative, you are outside **MY** premises. If you are positive, you are inside **MY** premises. **MY** premises now mean **The Holy Spirit** of **Truth** and **HE** has taken control of the whole world. That is the positive thoughts. Outside **MY** premises are the negative thoughts. They are all in your system. It is like you are in this world, but you are not of this world. So, you can have thoughts, which are positive or thoughts that are negative. All are in your heart.

The human system, as a body, as a man, as a human being is a nation of THE FATHER GOD, the human being is a universe. There is positive in you and there is also negative in you. If you accept the positive news inside you that is, the positive idea, which means that you accept this information. Then **I, THE FATHER GOD THE SUPREME ALTAR** will **ALTER** you and take over your system and the management of your life. That means from that moment you are inside you.

What is in you then becomes **THE FATHER GOD THE CREATOR OF THE UNIVERSE** as your inner self.

That will be the inside of you. However, any time you commit sin for instance, you think evil, you are annoyed and or you fight, you do something that is not fair, something that is not good for **MY SPIRIT**, then **I** become the outside of you.

When **I** become the outside of you for more than seventy-two hours, then the negative self that was outside comes in. It breaks through the barrier and comes in.

In you there is **outside self** and **inside self.** **I** have been using love to send the negative spirit away from the **inside** of man because love is the light. So, every human being now understands that inside of you there is outside and inside self. When you understand this bit then, you will know that you should and always have to think well, meaning to think only positive thoughts. You should speak well, meaning to speak positive and good words. You should hear well, meaning to hear only positive and good words and act well that is conduct yourself positively so that your positive self will always be in you.

If you do not think well, if you do not speak well and do not hear well and do well, then the negative self occupies you and that is when you have problems.

You should use this information – this Revelation Lecture to rebuke the negative self of you to stay away from inside of you. So that you will always think well, always do good things and have good instincts and good mission. Your attitude will always be nice and your environment will always be clean. You will always shine and the Light of **THE FATHER**

GOD will always be around you and the weather will always be good.

The winter in your heart is bad mood. When the sun shines outside of you that is, when the light is outside of you, the weather is bad and that is the bad mood. That is when you have annoyance. That is when you have bad feelings. That is when things spoil around you. When you have bad mood, a lot of things can go bad. Always allow **The Holy Spirit** to be in charge of your heart. Let in happiness, be joyous, sing songs, think well and speak well. Think positive thoughts, speak positive words, be good, feel fine and feel happy. Maintain **The Holy Spirit** in you and the weather will always be clear. You will always be in summer.

In summer, the road is clear. There is no bump. The environment is bright and nice. There is no damp when the summer is always around you. But when you allow the winter to be around you often, it is always *dampington* spirit. You will feel bad and things will be wrong around you.

How do you know how to conquer and keep yourself inside of you?
You should always to be in good spirit, have good mind and have love. Love conquers all evil.
Forgive one another.
Think well, speak well, hear well and act well.
Be positive in your thoughts and always read positive writs. Read the good books.
Read books about **THE FATHER GOD.** It has the potency to keep you inside of yourself and send the

negative self outside of you all the time just as **I** did after **I** sent Adam and Eve away from **MY** premises because of the spirit that **Altar** them. The only things that made **ME** come back as Jesus Christ using Adam's house was to send the negative self outside of mankind.

I came back on earth using Adam's spirit soul as reincarnated second Adam, the POSITIVE SELF and **I** finally sent out that **idiot spirit soul** away from Adam – away from mankind.

When **I** died on the cross, **I** said, *"It is finished."* That means from that moment **I** went back into man and lived as the Holy Potency in human beings. So, now **I AM** waiting for you, all humans! Every single one of you needs to come back to **ME,** your **CREATOR** – your **FATHER GOD.**

If you confess your sins and accept **ME, THE FATHER GOD, I** will live in you because **I AM** around all the time. Since that blood of Christ is always there, as the energy, avoid the unnecessary ritual of spilling blood of animals and any other blood for that matter.

When **I AM** not in you there is the risk of you procreating a subhuman. From the moment **I AM** not in you and a union occurs, meaning, the man and the woman fornicate, what actually manifests between the two of you is animal. One of three creatures' animal, bird or fish has taken root from your union to manifest physically as human-animal, human-bird or human-fish. It is not a real human being that will result from your union.

Many people seeming give birth to a human but do you know what you actually put to birth? You could have put to birth antelope, snake or monkey, fish of any type of creature or any specie of birds. You gave birth to anything but not a real human being. How many people give birth to a real human being?

If a serpent spirit soul or negative spirit soul say vampire, witchcraft is in you the man or in the woman you copulate with, what you will give birth to is that negative spirit in you or her that was at standby waiting for the opportunity to become human being. They are always at a standby, waiting and wanting to come to the world to cause trouble. All these human-animals, human-birds and human-fish are filled up everywhere in this world. That is the reason there are so many negativism, trouble, problems, wars, killings and all amount of negativism in the world.

The problems in the world are caused by these animals because they have been in the world millions and millions of years and not able to achieve anything positive like loving one another. They have no love in them and no unity. There is no oneness, no peace and they fight – a lot! Nothing good comes from them. These human-animals, human-birds and human-fish have the various animal instincts in them relative to their natural templates of the particular animal they are. Their behaviours demonstrate the sub-humans they are. Hence, they instigate wars and go to war. They kill, quarrel, fight and exhibit all other elementary behaviours.

I established good governments, good laws and good system to make the whole world to be good, which the negative ones ruin. The negative ones are all these human-animals, human-birds and human-fish that took control of the world and mess everything up. They do not allow any laws of God to stand. They go about formulating lots of ideas to pollute the world. They came up with Genetically Modified Food to pollute the entire humanity and the environment. They go about creating lots of things to cause wars and all sorts of problems in the whole world, all that is the result of low mentality in creation.

The real human God! When you see the real mankind the image and likeness of **THE FATHER GOD** – a positive child of God, when you see them, there is peace in them, there is love, there is harmony, there is oneness and there is every good thing in them and around them.

Until these sub-humans take evolution and subdue the negative **Altar** in them and allow the Supreme WORD to **Altar** them and give them new world, then their world and environments will never be good.

Therefore, be careful and be aware where the base of your operation is. Make sure you are positive. Think well, speak well, hear well and behave well to send the negative self away from your inside and attract **The Holy Spirit** into you.

Attract love, peace, humility, oneness, kindness and mercy into you. Attract all these good selves into you to be in yourself. When have these good virtues in you,

then all is well with you. Then you will have the flavour of **THE SUPREME WORD.**
THE SUPREME SPIRIT THE FATHER GOD will always be with you. That is how to put on Christ.

F: **YOUR POSITION OF LIFE AND DEAD SOUL REVEAL**

This Revelation Lecture reveals **The Position of Your Life And Your Death Soul Is Now Revealed.** What is your **Dead Soul**? **Dead Soul** is the negativism that lives in you.

Dead Soul is the negativism that controls you.

Dead Soul is the negativism that makes you to have the urge to be bad and to do bad things.

Dead Soul is the negativism that makes you to do wrong things.

Dead Soul is the negativism that makes you to think evil. It is the negativism that makes you hate people. **Dead Soul** is the negativism that makes you to even deny this WORD. This wonderful Revelation! You could say that you do not like the wonderful Revelation Lecture because of that **Dead Soul** in you. It is the **Dead Soul** in you that **Altar** you to hate all positive things.
I, THE FATHER GOD COMMAND THAT DEAD SOUL IN YOU TO BE OUT! FOR YOU TO LIKE POSITIVE THINGS FROM TODAY! FOR THIS WORD TO LIVE IN YOU TODAY!
I, COMMAND AND CAST AWAY DEAD SOUL FROM THE ENTIRE OF YOUR LIFE! **I** BUNDLED THEM AND IMPRISONED THEM SO THAT

YOU WILL BE FREE FROM THE DAY YOU ACCEPT THIS WORD AND **ME THE FATHER GOD**! You must accept this truth and say: **THANK YOU FATHER!** As soon as you say: **THANK YOU FATHER GOD!** - All negativisms that imprisoned you will vanish! You have done lots of things! You went everywhere looking for deliverance. Nobody can deliver you. Satan cannot deliver you. Do you know what Satan has done? Satan established so many churches and so many prayer houses. They are obviously façade that masked the evil activities in those places. When you go to them to deliver you they imprison you the more instead.

It is only yourself that will deliver you because you know your heart and what you feel. This is the only way of truth to deliver you. Do not go to anybody to infuse anything that you do not know the beginning and the end of, into you. Just read positive words and positive information. Pray to **THE FATHER GOD.** Kneel down wherever you are and knock your head on the ground and call the name and the blood of Christ. **The Supreme Energy** is the **Blood of Christ** that was sacrificed. **I, The Spoken WORD** came as second Adam and died for mankind.

So, use that energy to conquer demons in all its forms. You do not need any other sacrifice. All that you need to do is to preserve your good environment.

If you eat too much food and become heavy, it affects environment. Eating fish and meat, committing fornication and adultery, having annoyance in you and committing the rest of the sins, spoil the environment. Avoid all those things that when you involve with them would make your environment not to be good. As a result would attract the negative self to come into you. Witchcraft for instance, likes dirty places. It is evil. So avoid dirt to avoid such evil and indeed all evil.

I gave a Revelation Lecture about the basement human beings and that the actual technology came from water and it is not evil. The basement human beings are types of spirit souls of wealth that come to this world, as angels but in the form of human beings to create things that are good. Most of these human beings are spiritual and mystic people by birth. Therefore, positive science and scientific discoveries and the technology are knowledge from **THE FATHER GOD**.

What caused problem is that the witchcraft spirit soul– the negative spirit uses these scientific creations to cause war. These groups of people create things for good and positive uses. The negative ones use them instead for evil things and in negative ways. They misuse most of the scientific discoveries and technological inventions that are for good and positive uses.

Countries claim to defend themselves. What do you defend for? Can anyone defend his or her life or soul? Even if you have the best Army or an outstanding Police Force they are to help keep law and order in your country. Why do you go to other people's country to instigate war or to make war with them? These people have not come to your place to make war with you. Therefore, stay in your country and defend yourself. Everybody should practice *'Live and Let Live.'*

If you leave your territory to go to war with another country, that means you are claiming arrogance and pomposity. Those who elevate themselves **I** will reduce them! **I** will reduce them to nothing! If you do not humble yourself in this world and hear this **WORD** and stop claiming that you are powerful, **I** will debase you. Anyone or any country that exhibit arrogance and pomposity and goes to war with another country without a good reason, **I, THE FATHER GOD** will debase you. Those people you go to fight did not come to you for war.

If individuals go about killing people, find the person and arrest the person.
If you commit sin you will pay for your sin.
If you kill you shall be killed.
Do not go to destroy and kill innocent people in the name of war. In the name of one person you went and killed one million people. You will definitely pay for your action. In the name of being big you go and lord over other people. Why should you do that? Are you justified to go to war against someone who did not pose any threat of war with you?

If you are powerful and are so rich, protect your own country. Stay in your domain. Do not go to fight people and their country. Anyone that left his own or her own life to go and find trouble with another person, **I** will reduce that person to zero.

BELIEVE ME! THIS WORD IS COMING FROM THE **SUPREME WORD** OF THE UNIVERSE!

You know you command by the WORD but **THE SUPREME WORD** WILL supersede your order. Any order in this world that is inappropriate, **I THE FATHER GOD, THE SUPREME WORD OF THE UNIVERSE** will thwart it! What will you use to make the order?

There are three things that exist, the spirit, the soul and the physical. Who are those things? **I, THE FATHER GOD** is the SPIRIT. **I, THE FATHER GOD** is the WORD. **I, THE FATHER GOD** lives in you, man! I control the three capacities. Therefore, do not deviate from the order of love, peace, humility and the rest of the positive virtues of **THE FATHER GOD.**

Stay where you are and be what you want to be in your own place. Do not go to disturb another person.

If you do that and call your self "powerful" **I** will reduce you to nothing and you will never succeed with what you went to exact your power.

Do not forget that **I AM** SPIRIT! If therefore, you think that you can fight **ME THE SUPREME SPIRIT OF THE FATHER GOD ALMIGHTY**, or you think you are big and that you have money and can use your money to destroy the world, **I** will render you poor and useless.

If you use your physical power to go to suppress and undermine people, **I** will make you become weak.

If you use your wisdom and your knowledge to be wicked to people and to do bad things **I** will make you to become stupid.

If you use your wealth or your greatness to overpower people and to make people look stupid **I** will reduce you to become low and to zero.

If however, you use your wisdom, even your stupidity, even your weakness to help people, **I** will raise you up. **I** will make you rich.
I will make you wealthy.
I will make you powerful.
I will make you to control all things.

If you practice live and let live, **I** will make you live peacefully.

That is **MY ORDER AS THE SUPREME WORD OF THE UNIVERSE!**

I Altar the whole world. Let **ME** tell you the dweller on earth. In Heaven, in the soul and in the physical **I AM THE SUPREME ALTAR.**

I Altar Everywhere, Here and There, including every atmosphere, as well as the world that has not manifested and the World of Manifestation, **I Altar** them and control them. The more you look the less you see. **I AM *EVERYWHERE*, *HERE* and *THERE*.** Therefore, **Your Position of Live and Dead Soul Reveal** today.

Your **Dead Soul** is when you leave your life to go and disturb other people lives. You create a **Dead Soul** for yourself with such actions.

Your **Live Position** is when you live and let live. It is also when you forgive, when you think well and speak well; when you help people, when you love and when practice good things. That is your Life - **Your True Position Revealed** today. You must therefore, choose the one that you would like to be –**Live Position** or **Dead Soul**.

Every individual in all countries, all communities, all tribes, all clans, all families, indeed all human beings, your **True Position in Life Revealed** today, if you think you are whatsoever you are and if you know that you are strong ask yourself this question: What happened to previous strong people in the world?

Anything you vomited and you went back to swallow it, you have contaminated your system. No correct person would eat human waste, even if it were your own faeces.

When you eat, the good part of the food you eat remains in you. That is what you the male can pass to your female partner to create more of you. That good part of the food you ate formed the blood in you called semen.

A man gives the semen to a woman and that results in a child. That is because the system retained the positive part of the food you ate and rejected the bad part. This good part absorbed by the body formed blood, which then form semen. The semen then forms a child inside the woman. In the same token, The **WORD** takes the spirit, in the form of what you think, what you understand and how you understand life, your practises, your level, your labour and your mind. The spirit takes all of them including that of your wife to be the content of the child both of you will bear.

The SPIRIT, the life in you also processes all the food you eat everyday. It will then take the positive part as blood energy to form the child you will give birth to. That is the progress of birth and continuation of your offspring. That is also where you will come back to in your next rebirth on earth. So, your **Life** and your **Death** are in your hands and shall be revealed today. That also is your soul.

If you want to be happy in the Supreme Future, be happy now.
If you want to be rejoicing in the Supreme Future, rejoice now.
Create your happiness now for tomorrow.
Create your joy.
Create your environment now for tomorrow.

Did you not take a picture of yourself when you were young? Now you look at it to remember how you were young. Even though you are old or older now compared to you in that picture, you still look young and will always look young as far as that picture is concerned. Your youthful image in that picture will never change. A similar thing is applicable here, if you want to enjoy tomorrow, create it today so that that joy will remain in the memory for you tomorrow. If you want to be rich, help people. Anything you have, share it with people. The riches you shared with people will still remain for you tomorrow.

Any good thing you want tomorrow, do it today. Practice it. Practical Christianity is what you need. It is the practicing of good

things. Christ means The KING of Kings and the LORD of Lords.
Do good things and good things will follow you. Do bad things and bad follows you. That is the position of your soul. Let the inside of you be positive and not negative. When you do this, you have now created a positive situation for your future and that will manifest for you.
This is an OPEN BOOK not a Secret Book again. This is OPEN WISDOM.

G: **THE CAUSE OF YOUR POSITIVE AND NEGATIVE INSTINCTS, EMOTIONAL ACTIONS AND SENSATIONS**
This aspect is to do with your resources, spiritual, physical and otherwise.

When you attach yourself to positive, be careful about what you think, what you speak, what you hear and your actions because all of them form the energy of your future life or your soul improvement. They aid to form the energy around the facilities you are growing.

For instance, if you build a beautiful house as you are young and have the money that is where you will live comfortably when you get old. If on the contrary, you frittered all your money away in frivolous living and fruitless ventures when you were young and had money, you have done yourself great disservice now that you are old and your retirement life does not look rosy. You no longer have money to do anything substantial like building a good house for yourself. In such situation, you would not say you did not have the money to build yourself a beautiful house because you did.

You entered into secret society and killed people. You will not be comfortable in your life because when you are supposed to enjoy that is when the spirit soul of those people you killed would come to haunt you, just like the spirit soul of Abel that haunts Cain.
Every killer, every wicked person - you should know that the souls of those you killed and are wicked to will haunt you. They will not let you have rest. No matter how you sacrificed, no matter the degree of craftiness you employ to avert them, no matter the bribe you offered, it won't stop the souls from haunting you.
You killed someone and went back to buy them over by offering

money. The bribes you offered will not work again. All negative ideas have been exposed and the energy is dead. You will reap exactly what you sowed now on this earth and the time to come.

The Cause of Your Positive and Negative Instincts, Emotional actions and Sensations are in your hands to correct them now. Sing songs of praises and glory to **THE FATHER GOD**.
Take this Lecture Revelation to your soul.
Be happy!
Be positive!
Be forgiving all the time.
Then you will see that the Positive Holy Spirit of **THE FATHER GOD** would **altar** you. **I, THE FATHER GOD, THE SUPREME NATURE, THE SUPREME HOLY SPIRIT** will be in harmony with you. **I** will

always be with you and live in you because your environment is good.

There are some friends you have that always come to your house because you receive them well. You cook good food and entertain them well. If your friends were positive, they would share with your positive spirit soul.

They type of friends you have is according to the type of life you live. If you live positive life, positive people will like to come to your house and be friendly with you. If you live negative life, negative people will like to keep company with you. For instance, when you drink and get drunk and also when you fornicate and gossip, the people that are drunk and fornicate and gossip will always keep you company. They will like you because you have something in common to share with them.

If you are someone who does not welcome gossip, you do not drink, you do not smoke, you do not fornicate, you do not generally lead carnal live you will be an isolated person in the community. People will not bother with you. If someone mentions your name they would respond – ah leave that one he is holy-holy person. They could even say you are Satan because you do not share with their kind of life. You should not mind.
Be yourself.
Live by your conscience.
Do not live according to how people want you to live because salvation is by the individual. Your salvation is independent of everyone. Lead a positive life so that all will be well with you.

If you live a sanitized life **I, THE SANITIZED SPIRIT** will come and live in you and manifest **MY** glory in you and you will seed **THE FATHER GOD'S** glory in earnest.

CONCLUSION A: **THE DOOR TO YOUR SOUL**

The Door To Your Soul Is Your Heart. Your system is also the door into your soul.

How something gets into you is through your mind and through words. It can also be through what you eat including what you wear. Who you surrender your heart to and also the person you welcome into your innersole is vital to your life. Therefore, be careful whom you welcome into your heart, what you think and what you accept. When evil people present something and you accept their idea that means they have got into your life and soul.

The door to your soul is your heart. As soon as you give your heart to somebody or you can allow someone to come into you and live your life, the person has access into your soul. You could be living your life, but you would not know that someone is living your life for you and controlling you.

Why not give your heart to **THE FATHER GOD THE CREATOR OF THE UNIVERSE.** Why not give your heart to this **WORD, THE SUPREME WORD OF THE UNIVERSE.**

Join in the celebration of the **SUPREME WORD.** It is a universal celebration program to honour and appreciate the **WORD** titled: *THE UNIVERSAL*

SUPREME WORD SEASON CELEBRATION.
Give all your life to **THE FATHER GOD.**
Love **THE FATHER GOD** more than anything else in your life. Let **THE FATHER GOD** be first thing in your memory. Let the positive **WORD** – this **WORD**, the Word of Love (**I** don't mean the love of man and woman), the love of peace be inside you.
Have the Love of God in you.
Have the love of good thinking.
Have the love of doing good things.
Have the love of being nice.
Have the love of kindness.
Have the love of practising good life.
Have the love of helping one another and being positive.
When you have all that love in you, you have opened the door for

THE SUPREME ALTAR OF THE FATHER GOD, THE HOLY SPIRIT OF TRUTH to **ALTER** and **ALTAR** you. As a result, your environment will be wonderful! - Even here now and later and in time to come.

That is it - **The Door To Your Soul Is Your heart.** What you accept is what causes you to think good or bad thoughts. What you admire is responsible for your thoughts whether good or bad thoughts and also what you talk about.

Talk about what is good.

Think about what is good.

Do not entertain anything that is not good. Rebuke it! Erase it away from your memory so that you will be free!

CONCLUSION B: NEGATIVE IN AND OUT – THE FORNICATION ACT OF SEXUALITY

Another way that evil, witchcraft, Satan - all sorts of nonsense can get into the human system is through the acts of fornication. If you fornicate you are eating what is bad. Sexuality is the sensation of evil. It was the spirit of sexuality that the serpent used that to deceive Eve and Eve in turn used it to deceive Adam. Sexuality is the influence of negativism including that of witchcraft. All witchcraft, all the people that go about collecting people's star and are wicked to people, use sexuality, during that time of sexual sensation, it coils from your feet up and enter inside you like snake and take all the good things inside you and run away. That is what evil people do. However, a positive child of **THE FATHER GOD** with the Power of the Holy Spirit and the Word of God in them cannot fall victim.

If you have the Word of God in you, a woman or man that is negative that comes to commit sexual acts with you cannot stand you and so runs away. This is so because as soon as they come closer to you, **I SUPREME FATHER GOD, THE SUPREME ALTAR** would **ALTAR** you during the whole period.

If you are not positive and you force yourself onto a positive person and tempt this positive child of God, **I THE SUPREME ALTAR** will **ALTAR** this positive child of God.

That is the reason that sometimes a woman you had a "lovely" chat with would not want to come to see you again, so also a man. If you asked to know the reason he or she would say oh forget about it. What they would not tell you is that they have tested you and could not get you so they left you alone.

They would become annoyed with you and would leave you alone because they were not able to take your spirit soul. You spirit soul did not respond to them and so they were not able to take your spirit soul. This only occurred because you are positive with the power of the Holy Spirit of **THE FATHER GOD**.

The same thing happens if you have negative spirit soul inside you and a positive person comes to you. He or she will run away because they could not stand you.

This is the fight going on in the world now.

Transmission of evil is via the WORD and also through the acts of sexuality that is, fornication. That is what happens. That is the meaning of Tree of Life and Tree of Death. How do you conquer all these things?

Use the **Word of God** to conquer.
Use the **Word of Life**.
Use your mind
Use your heart to direct positivism into your inner self. That is the **Altar.** That is that you have allowed **THE SUPREME SPIRIT OF GOD** to **ALTAR** you and take charge of your life.

If you are positive and travelled to anywhere and they are predominantly negative people, they would not have anything to do with you. **THE FATHER**

GOD, THE POSITIVE ENERGY, THE LIGHT OF GOD THE FORCE OF HOLY SPIRIT will surround you and all those negative people will run away from you.

If however, the embodiment of God is not in you then you are weak. If you happen to be around the negative people and you go to them they will capture you. So, think about this and know exactly how you open your mind, the type of word and the type of instructions you accept into you including the type of people you associate with. That was what happened to Adam and Eve. They were overtaken by evil because they were weak.

When **I** extracted that spirit soul out of Adam and kept it separate, how did Lucifer cunningly entered back into Adam and become one?

That made all negatives spirits to manifest on earth.

In that same notion, if **I** happen to use somebody's soul to recreate you or to transmit in you or to correct you, anytime you went back to sleep with that person and fornicate with him or her, you have gone back to reintroduce that spirit back into your inner life soul. If it was negative spirit soul that **I** extracted from the person and you went back and slept and fornicated with that person, then the negative spirit soul has been reintroduced into that person. This is one of the reasons **I** warned Ikouwem that he should be careful with his other self. **I** used the spirit of Mfon to recreate Mfon. So, if any day Ikouwem who is now a new soul goes back to have union with the old soul Mfon and they become one again, whatsoever happens as result is not **MY** business. That was the exact thing that happened with Adam and Eve.

When **I** called Adam into deep sleep and took one rib of Adam and created Eve, **I** did extraction. But Lucifer saw that **I** had extracted her from Adam, she went back and pretended she loved Adam and Eve too much and cunningly reintroduced that spirit back into Adam. That became the downfall of mankind. But who will die again, now? **I,** The higher self of Adam Our Lord Jesus Christ has died once and for all. So, that is that.

CONCLUSION C: **POSITIVE IN AND OUT IS THE WORD**

You now know that your heart is the door to your soul that is, your inner self door. How do you open this door for either negative or positive to get inside you? First of all it is via the WORD.

When you hear something as you are hearing this Lecture Revelation now if it sounds positive in your ear – even suppose you are a negative person or you are witchcraft or you entered secret society, you kill or you are wicked and you know in yourself that you are not a good person and you are guilty of all bad things you are accused guilty of, but you open your heart to this **SUPREME WORD** and you accepts this **WORD** of **DIVINE INFORMATION** and confessing all your guiltiness then you will be free of all your sins.

Do not forget that **THE WORD** is **THE CREATOR,**
THE WORD is **THE FATHER GOD. THE WORD** does

everything, but **THE WORD** is divided in to two.
The back of **THE SUPREME WORD** is negative.
The front of **THE SUPREME WORD** is positive.
So, accept the **FRONT,** which is the **TRUTH.** THE FRONT MEANS THE TRUTH.
The back means lie; it means something that does not exist. The back means something that is not truthful.
That is darkness. ACCEPT THE **FRONT**, IT IS THE **LIGHT**.
This one is your homework.
Start accepting the front. When you start doing this, then you are accepting this WORD. It then follows that you are accepting the good words and rejecting all the negative words because you know in your heart that this WORD is positive. That is the reason you

accepted it. Think about it. The WORD **HIMSELF** will then analyze **HIMSELF** in you.

As you are hearing this now, if this WORD is evil word or ordinary word or whatsoever, it will analyze itself in you because the **WORD** is there in you.

The Natural Positive Spirit of Life is in your heart to analyze **HIMSELF** in you since **HE** is the Magnetic Force of Energy in your heart.

I AM TALKING TO YOU NOW VIA THIS WORD. **I** WILL ANALYZE **MYSELF** IN YOU. **I** WILL CONFIRM IT THAT THIS WORD IS FROM **ME THE FATHER GOD.**
IT IS TRUE WORD.
IT IS THE WORD OF LIFE
IT IS THE WORD OF TRUTH.
IT IS THE WORD THAT YOU MUST OPEN UP TO. If you open

the door of your heart and of your soul to this **SUPREME WORD**, then **I** will come into you and change the environment of whatsoever situation you are in for good! **I** will also protect you against evil!

When you have accepted **ME, THE FATHER GOD** by accepting this positive WORD, this positive idea and launch this WORD in your heart, then the other things that live in you and are not consistence with the positive WORD will find their way out and will leave you one by one.

Whether they like it or not they will surely leave you. When you render them redundant, they will find you no longer useful to them. They are not useful to you again because -

Gossiping - NO MORE!

Thinking evil – NO MORE!
Speaking evil - NO MORE!
Hearing of evil –NO MORE!
To engage in any negative - NO MORE!
Trying to kill - NO MORE!
Wickedness in you - NO MORE!
All those bad and wicked things - NO MORE!
You have rendered all those evil souls useless and redundant and they have left you. They have died natural death inside your heart and you have become a new person with a new environment.
What will come out from you now and after now and in the future will be good and you will become fine. That is the meaning of **Positive IN and OUT.**
THIS IS THE WORD OF **THE FATHER GOD**.
This is when you can invite **THE FATHER GOD, THE**

SUPREME ALTAR to **ALTER** you and live in you.
Use this as an OPEN BOOK OF LIFE to change for good and your future soul will be happy that **THE FATHER GOD** is directing you. Then the environment of your life becomes rearranged human being. You will continue to enjoy and live happily on this earth, in the Name of Our Lord Jesus Christ. Amen!

Let **my** peace and blessing abide with the entire world, now and forever, more. Amen!

THANK YOU FATHER

KING SOLOMON SPIRITUAL LIBRARY

THE GOD ENCYCLOPAEDIA WORD OF INFINITY

===========

King Solomon Spiritual Library, God Universal Information Centre Father's Talk (God Present)

WITH LOVE

Covered: This BOOK, e-book, software or software's, books, website, video, audio, idea or ideas, formula or formulas, manual or instruction manual.

... Hereby gives you a non-exclusive license to use the ... (THIS BOOK).
Some of the word here is coded with the (WORD OF SUPER HOLY AND INTELLIGENCE FATHER GOD ALMIGHTY)

Title, ownership rights, and intellectual property rights in and to the Website, Books, E-book, Audios and Videos, Shops and Store – e-Stores, Fundraisings, Celebrations and the supreme word seasons Celebration formulas and arrangement, Positive Inspiration, Holy (Fata), FATHER GOD ALMIGHTY POSSESSING SPIRIT in thought, in words and in did, thinking well, speaking well, hearing well and doing well shall remain in me and in ... The BOOK is protected by international copyright.

FATHER'S TALK (GOD PRESENT)

The message in The Father's Talk (GOD PRESENT) does not challenge any authority either individuals, groups or governments of any land or even any belief of any form. It is rather challenging the truth that is hidden from mankind. Therefore, any spirit, soul or physical human being who decides to challenge this truth shall have himself or herself to blame.

Key A

Any individual that reads any of The Father's Talk (GOD PRESENT) with faith; love and acceptance will experience immediate positive change in his or her life from spirit, soul to physical. If he or she accepts the message then he or she will be free from any evil.

Key B: **PEACE AND LOVE**
If you do not believe the contents of any of The Father's Talk (GOD PRESENT) it is possible through The Father's divine love and peace simply hands over your copy to a friend or somebody else that would like to keep a copy, or signing out from any of the website that connected to The Father's Talk (GOD PRESENT) KING SOLOMON SPIRITUAL e-LIBRARY without any evil and negative comments and you are blessed and free.

=========

FROM THE DESK OF INSPIRATIONAL HEAD
Fees, Prices and Donations;
There is no refund on fees, price or donations since your fees price

or donations are using as a charity contribution to do administration work of THE SUPREME WORD, So please kindly read this first before you decide to involves yourself in any of the under mention of HRM King Solomon David Jesse ETE universal Inspirational Businesses of (GOD PRESENT) in cash, kinds and otherwise.

I CAME FROM THE FATHER GOD, WITH THE FATHER GOD, AND BY THE FATHER GOD TO ESTABLISH THE FOLLOWING:

Therefore, all distributors and contributors of The Father's Talk (GOD PRESENT), The Spiritual Advice, Healing and Counselling on General Live (The Universal Supreme Spiritual General Hospital), New Songs and Psalms of King David and Solomon, The

Word of **GOD** Processing City in Ikot Okwo or e-City online, The Trinity Celebration, **"OUC FUND"**, The Universal Bank Account For All Creations, **"ERUFA"** ETE Royal Universal Family, **"THEUNISAL-SUREME SEACELION"** The Universal Supreme Word Season Celebration To Appreciates THE FATHER GOD ALMIGHTY **"THEUNI-SUREME WORA THECRO-THEUNISE" The Universal Supreme Word Almighty, THE CREATOR OF THE UNIVERSE** should attach this information to all readers, website visitors, distributors, affiliates person/group, celebrant and celebrations centres, supporters and promoters, members, workers and voluntary workers, Ete royal universal palace committee, governments and many other centres as an agreement. Please kindly know that I am not answering to any physical human except **PEACE, UNITY AND LOVE.**

"THEUNISAL-SUREME WORA THECRO-THEUNISE".

I AM IN THE STAGE OF SUPER HOLY AND INTELLIGENCE FATHER GOD POSITIVE MADNESS OF THE HOLY SPIRIT OF TRUTH, ENYEN ODUDU ODUDU ODUDU ABASI MI OOO ZIM ZIM ZIM ASSASU, POSITIVE POSITIVE POSITIVE. UKEMEKE AKA IDIOK UNAM. Let the peace and blessing of the Holy Father abide with everybody who corporate with this divine Father's Talk (GOD PRESENT

**BY
THE HOLY SPIRIT OF THE
FATHER GOD
THROUGH HIS SERVANT**
Senior Christ Servant
HRM King Solomon David Jesse
ETE
Brotherhood of the
Cross and STAR
Eteroyal Universal family
Ikot Okwo
The Great City of Refuge,
Ete Community
Ikot Abasi LGA-543001
Akwa Ibom State Nigeria-W/A
Tel. 08036693841
Email:
ksslibrary@eteroyalmail.com
www.kingsolomonspirituallibrary.com
www.thewordcity.com
www.come4word.com
www.theinfinityword.com

READ AT LEAST SEVEN LECTURE'S REVELATIONS BEFORE YOU CAN MAKE ANY COMMENTS
In the Name of Our Lord Jesus Christ In the Blood of Our Lord Jesus Christ
Now and forever more
Everybody should have access and read at least seven **FATHER'S TALK (GOD PRESENT)** Lecture's Revelations before you can make any comments about it. If you do not go through at least seven **FATHER'S TALK** lectures and you comment you may make mistakes. When you make mistakes your blood will be upon you because you would have taken voluntary evolution to misquote **THE FATHER GOD THE CREATOR OF THE**

UNIVERSE. If however, you go through any seven of **THE FATHER'S TALK (GOD PRESENT)** – one of **THE FATHER'S TALK** stands for one Spirit of God, which means that **FATHER'S TALK GOD PRESENT** Lectures Revelation are witness by the Seven Spirits of God, which **I** use as the Seven Church of God and Seven days of the Week, Seven spirits of Creations in one Supreme energy of THE FATHER GOD, THE SPOKEN WORD. When you read seven **FATHER'S TALK** Lectures then, **I THE FATHER GOD** will reveal you as positive person. Then you will have a portion in **ME**. One of **THE FATHER'S TALK** will have a portion in you. Then you would know that this information came from **THE FATHER GOD.**

The Father's Talk God Present is not a mere talk from a mere man!
In the Name of Our Lord Jesus Christ In the Blood of Our Lord Jesus Christ
Now and forever more

THE UNIVERSAL SUPREME ACKNOWLEDGEMENT

'THE ONLY SOURCE AND REMEDY TO END ALL HUMANITIES PROBLEMS'

> Join me to Celebrate;
> Acknowledge,
> Appreciates and give full
> RECOGNITION to
> THE UNIVERSAL
> SUPREME WORD,
> YOUR LIFE FORCE,
> THE TOTALITY OF
> ALL TOTALITIES
> YOUR CREATOR,
> THE FATHER GOD
> ALMIGHTY,
> THE CREATOR OF
> THE UNIVERSE

WWW.COME4WORD.COM
Contact EMAIL:
hrmkingsolomon@eteroyalmail.com
THANK YOU FATHER

The title List of some of the
Father's Talk
(GOD Present)

1: THE MANUAL OF THE SPOKEN WORD

2: THE MANUAL OF LIFE

3: INVESTMENT WITH GOD

4: ISO IBOT EDEM IBOT

5: THE CHARACTER OF THE NEW WORLD

6: HELPMANTRANS

7: UNDERSTANDING MY WORD

8: TRUTH, POSITION, POST AND NAME

9: NON STOP BLESSING

10: IMPRESSION

11: STAGES OF EDUCATIONS (SPE, SSE & SUE)

12: THE ENGINEERING OF LIFE

13: THE CONTENT PACKAGE

14: THE BUDGET OF THE NEW WORLD

15: DIVINE ATTENTION

16: THE BABY SPIRIT

17: PROMOTION

18: ADVANCE AND PROGRESSING MIND

19: THE TEMPLE OF THE LIVING GOD

20: I AM OK

21: THE SPIRIT OF TRUTH

22: THE PERFECT PERMANENCY

23: THE FATHER GOD, GOD, GOD THE FATHER

24: HUSBAND, WIFE AND CHILD

25: GOD AND HIS HARBINGER

26: LIFE EVERLASTING

27: POSSESS

28: MY MIND AND MY PLAN

29: AFTER HEART AND AFTER MIND

30: MY DECLARATION & STAND IN BCS

31: BEYOND THE HOPE OF FAITH

32: MENTAL STAIN

33: THE PRINCIPLE OF SELF HOLD

34: THE MASTERSHIP

35: HIDU-CUM

36: THE UNIVERSAL PARENT

37: ADVANCED YOU AND ME

38: THE GREAT UNIVERSAL CHANGE

39: THE PROJECTED MIND

40: INDESTRUCTIBLE BLESSED FIVE STARS

41: ASTROTS, GOD PRESENT I AND MY FATHER

42: SONGS THE COMPLETION

43: THE RIGHT BUTTON

44: <u>AKWA ABASI IBOM- ETE - DIRECTING NDITO AKWA IBOM</u>

45: THE DIGITAL AGE

46: <u>GOD IS OFFICIAL CHAMPION</u>

47: A TRUE WITNESS

48: MYSTERY OF PROCREATION AND BIRTH

49: <u>THE UNIVERSAL UMBRELLA</u>

50: THE FORERUNNER

51: A OF A TO Z (FIRST OF ALL)

52: MAN IN THREE CAPACITIES

53: THE TRUE LIFE OF HOLY SPIRIT PERSONIFIED

54: IN-BETWEEN THE FATHER & THE SON

55: DIVINE ARRANGEMENT & AUTHORITY

56: TWENTY FIRST CENTURY IS NOT FOR SATAN

57: THE SUPREME WORD SEASON CELEBRATION

58: THE MAXIMUM DEITY

59: TRANSFORMER TRANSMITTER AND WAVE

60: THE SUPREME FUTURE

61: THE BYLOVE OF WORD

62: THE SIGNATURE OF THE FATHER GOD

63: THE TWO WAYS

64: THE UNDERSTANDING OF LIFE

65: THE GREATER THAN SOLOMON IS HERE

66: THE CONQUEROR

67: THE SPIRITUAL GENERAL INSPECTOR OF LIFE

68: THE NIGERIA IN THE AFRICA
Part one

69: THE NIGERIA IN THE AFRICA
Part two

70: THE CREATOR AND CREATIONS PART ONE

71: THE CREATOR AND CREATIONS PART TWO

72: THE CREATOR AND CREATIONS PART THREE

73: THE SUPREME TEACHER

74: THE SPIRITUAL COVER

75: THE NIGERIA IN THE AFRICA PART THREE

76: THE SUPREME BELIEVE

77: CAST AND BAN (LECTURE IN LIVERPOOL)

78: LIFE EXTENSION MANUAL

79: THE SPIRITUAL TRAFFIC

80: THE VOICE OF THE CREATOR

81: MY OFFICE

82: LIFE SPIRITUAL FIRE EXTINGUISHER

83: INFORMATION

84: FATHER GOD FINAL ARRANGEMENT

85: THE LOVERS OF CHRIST

86: I LOVE YOU, I LOVE YOU TOO

87: THE UNIVERSAL SUPREME UPDATE

88: THE SUPREME ALTAR

THANK YOU FATHER

www.ingramcontent.com/pod-product-compliance
Lightning Source LLC
Chambersburg PA
CBHW020738230426
43665CB00009B/478